A FRESH LOOK AT IMPROVING YOUR WORK ENVIRONMENT

Using Project Management Principles

STEVE HOUSEWORTH, PhD, PMP

iUniverse, Inc.
Bloomington

A Fresh Look at Improving Your Work Environment
Using Project Management Principles

iUniverse books may be ordered through booksellers or by contacting:

iUniverse
1663 Liberty Drive
Bloomington, IN 47403
www.iuniverse.com
1-800-Authors (1-800-288-4677)

Because of the dynamic nature of the Internet, any web addresses or links contained in this book may have changed since publication and may no longer be valid. The views expressed in this work are solely those of the author and do not necessarily reflect the views of the publisher, and the publisher hereby disclaims any responsibility for them.

Any people depicted in stock imagery provided by Thinkstock are models, and such images are being used for illustrative purposes only.

Certain stock imagery © Thinkstock.

ISBN: 978-1-4620-5623-1 (sc)
ISBN: 978-1-4620-5624-8 (e)

Library of Congress Control Number: 2011917534

Printed in the United States of America

iUniverse rev. date: 11/2/2011

TABLE OF CONTENTS

LIST OF TABLES

List of Figures

Introduction: Adding Value

My focus for this book is combining both the principles of project management and the work ethic needed to make it effective. This is what I am calling a "value-added work environment" and sometimes a "project management work environment".

My perspective is that all the work performed in your organization is to add value. This could be value through maintaining the status quo, communicating a new human resource policy, winning a contract, research and development or cleaning the stairwell. Project management principles are about completing <u>your</u> work and adding value by using formalized processes, steps, rules, metrics, controls, etc.

Even though I am an experienced project manager and a huge advocate for project management, I need to say that <u>no organization</u> **needs** <u>project management</u>.

Hear me out before you ask for a refund.

Certainly, cleaning the stairwell does not entail detailed formal processes and metrics. It does benefit from instilling an ethic to provide value to your organization. Similarly, organizations <u>that have instituted</u> project management, Lean, Six Sigma, ISO 9000, etc. <u>don't always use these systems with an ethic to provide value.</u> If not managed properly their use regresses to a prescriptive, "follow the steps" level rather than a "let's use these to add value" level. Project management principles simply provide a structure for work, but <u>the implementation and execution depends on the ethic in your organization</u> to use the structure for the purpose of adding value.

Now, every organization has some type and level of formal structure and work ethic. Some are effective, some aren't. So, if your organization already has an established structure and an accompanying ethic that is effective to complete quality work, then you are already benefiting from a strong value-added work environment. However, the converse of this can go three ways:

1. Eager staff that wants to add value but does not have a formal structure to channel their dedication effectively. Project management principles can provide the channeling structure.

2. Formal work structure principles but not the value-added work ethic.

3. Either of the two above but which uses project management principles only for "projects". They don't extend the principles to work that aren't defined as projects.

I've worked within each organization. Eager staff whose efforts are not supported by a an effective work structure can become frustrated and lose their dedication; their value-added ethic. Staff without the value-added ethic can follow a formal work structure but omit simple, yet key features that make the difference between adding value and creating problems. The third situation is addressed specifically below in the sections: "Planning Knows No Bounds" and "Use Change Management Wherever Change Happens".

Think of a value-added work environment similar to formal accounting and formal human resources rules and policies. The formal structure, rules and processes provides uniformity, consistency, a common vocabulary, definitions, etc. so that everyone knows how to submit expense receipts or rules for taking sick time. The formal structure of project management actually facilitates completing work. The ethic of adding value needs to permeate the formal structure.

So, while no organization **needs** project management, if your organization wants to ensure that value is added by completing work with quality, then a formalized project management work environment ensures the value add. I'm aware that skepticism exists and that skeptics could say: "Sure! I'd like to see that!" Maybe even:

"Especially in this place." OK. Read on. A healthy skepticism usually surfaces meaningful issues. Hopefully, I address many adequately in this book

This book is about improving your work environment so that employees, vendors and clients know both

1. **The formal work structure / operations and**

2. **How they should work within it to add value to your organization**.

Years ago, when I first thought of this book I shared the concept with a colleague who asked "Do you mean creating a Project Management Office?" "No" I replied. A project management office (PMO) is a unit or office within an organization that structures and implements project management. I've seen strengths and weaknesses of formal project management in organizations with and without PMOs. Similar to having accounting and human resources departments, having a PMO may be a step in the right direction, but it is neither necessary nor sufficient to ensure completing work that adds value.

Now, this book complements my other book "Project Management for Executives and Those Who Want to Influence Executives" which presents the role of executives for actively supporting projects so that they add value. Using both books will provide a strong foundation for success. Both books are written intentionally concise to address specific topics and to be easy to use references.

Part of helping add value is providing active exercises and development steps that you can use in your organization. Many are presented at appropriate points in each chapter. To support this goal I have two recommendations. First, <u>read this book one chapter at a time taking notes and thinking of pros and cons</u>. Then brainstorm ideas. The first Appendix is a work table you can use for this purpose. I recommend keeping your finger in this page and looking at the table now. Create your own and keep your notes stuffed in the pages like a bookmark for each reference.

A second recommendation is to <u>consider the book as a reference source</u> that you can return to as you think of ideas or encounter situations and think "I know Houseworth mentioned this." Or, I want to share this with Renee because I think it fits her situation". So, while I present several active exercises and advocate several ways to implement into your organization, I encourage you to use this table – or create your own.

Section 1: Foundations

Chapter 1:   The Work Environment

The Ethic

My goal is to describe how to create an ethic within your organization so that <u>everyone understands how work should be structured to add value to the organization</u>. Secretaries, administrators, executives, business analysts, architects, electricians, etc. would be able to recognize things like:

- **Risks**
- **Changes**
- **Cost and Quality**
- **Planning and Scheduling**

Here are a few sample scenarios:

Risk scenario:

Fred sees something that seems odd. "I need to read the work order one more time to be sure it means what I think it does. OK, I was right and I see problems if I complete the work order "as is". Seems that not everything was thought through. Hmmm, this work order presents several risks that if they happen can mean serious issues. I guess this is a good time to see if my boss and his boss are serious that part of my role and responsibility as an employee is to raise these concerns."

Comment: In this example, the work culture should empower, encourage and reward Fred for raising these risks. Even if they eventually don't amount to anything. Fred is about to find out if the work culture supports him. How would people in your organization evaluate management's support to prevent risks? Also, see the section in Chapter 10 about the value of finding defects early. A sample tool is provided that helps evaluate cost savings.

Change scenario:

Irene is walking back to her desk thinking: "I just attended a meeting where executives insisted that two new features be added to our product by next month. The product has been under development for two years. No one on the project team dared to challenge the executives, but these changes are minor "nice to haves". If they are so important they should have been known and added long ago. Adding them now will take at least six months – not one. Bummer because, every month delay is costing us $100K of missed opportunity."

Comment: The work culture should constrain executives from doing this and should empower, encourage and reward others to challenge this type of action. In this example, the executive sponsor of the project is in an excellent position to protect the project from these unnecessary scope changes. In fact the value of executives understanding how they can support projects is the reason why I wrote the companion book, "Project Management for Executives and those who want to Influence Executives."

Cost and Quality scenario:

Norm is incredulous at what is happening: "I can't believe what I'm seeing. We electricians wired three floors before the drywall was installed, per the work sequence. Now, the crew cutting holes for outlet boxes are cutting through the drywall too deep, severing our wires. What a waste and cost increase because fixing this will take longer than the original wiring installation. Quality is going to be compromised by splicing the wiring to fix it. This means electricians will need to return to fix a problem we did not create before we can install the outlet boxes." "I have to stop this from getting worse."

Comment: The drywall installers are operating with a limited view of their job: "Get in, get out, get paid"; rather than an overall view of the value their job adds to the organization. Even if the drywall installers and electricians are vendors who are just executing their work orders, the work culture of their companies and the culture that develops contracts between companies, should empower, encourage and reward people to ensure that their one job is viewed within the total value of the work.

Planning and Scheduling scenario:

Robert came across several design documents that Jill posted to the project folder that were not expected at this stage of work. He decides to ask. "Jill, you're already working on designs and developing test cases? Aren't you supposed to submit the client's initial work request to the project manager so that we can plan and schedule the work before we begin designs?"

Jill: "Oh, that will just take too much time. Besides, all that planning stuff sounds good, but the client will just keep dragging their feet and we'll end up working evenings and weekends for the last two months, just like the last time. We didn't have a schedule nor did we plan the work then either. I'm the unit supervisor, so I don't have to follow that project process stuff."

Comment: See the slogan in Chapter 3 "Just because people are busy does not mean they are productive". Jill is potentially creating a lot of rework by making assumptions regarding designs and requirements for tests. Without the designs and detailed requirements the final solution and necessary tests can be quite different. Everyone in the organization should be willing to structure and plan work to ensure that the right work is planned and is performed as scheduled. Adjustments can always be made along the way, but planned and scheduled work allows adjustments to be controlled rather than uncontrolled. In fact, employees with higher levels of responsibility, like a unit supervisor, should be positive examples for others rather than negative examples.

I actually worked with people like Jill who knew that not planning or scheduling work would lead to problems, but they pushed ahead anyway – bouncing from one crises to the next like riding a wild stallion and complaining every moment about the situation they created. A central point here is that everyone can identify the right things to do, if they are provided the right structured environment and reinforcement. From secretaries to contract employees to research engineers, a project management oriented work environment can be used by all.

Development Exercise: I want to give you something to think about while you read. May even be a reinforcement exercise you can use with co-workers and friends.

You've probably heard this definition of insanity:

Insanity = Repeatedly doing things the same way and expecting different results.

Well, I changed the statement a bit. Think about what term or label would fit this statement.

? What term = Repeatedly doing things the same way and knowing this causes problems anyway.

Environments are not isolated

Notice that each of the above scenarios involved the work environment across management levels, business units and internal or external companies. This may not be a big surprise to you, but I've found that many companies don't evaluate these factors in creating or improving their work environment ethic. Often, organizations let the work ethic evolve on their own, assume that vendors or clients will focus on the overall good, etc. My point is that while building a positive-oriented project management work environment you will:

- Need to incorporate organizational structures and tools to mature this ethic.
- Need to incorporate methodologies to guide employees as they plan and complete work.

- Need to develop ways to partner with other organizations to complete work.

- Need to develop metrics to measure progress and direct your organization to the next steps along the maturation road.

Each of these topics are addressed in this book. Some are in distinct chapters and sections. Some are woven in with other subject matter, indicative of the interactive and integrative nature of project management.

Project management structure becomes self reinforcing

The more a formal, structured process for accomplishing work is used, i.e. a project management structure, the more everyone in your organization will begin to use the same vocabulary, set the same expectations, analyze work similarly, plan for success and expect others to plan for success. I want to contrast two organization frameworks to reinforce this point.

Table 1: Structured vs Unstructured Organizations

Unstructured Organization	Structured Organization
In this organization only projects use a set structure for the work and, even this is often shortcut when time or costs were pressed by those with authority. "Come on, let's get started. Don't worry that the project is not fully defined or authorized. We can do as much as possible until the executives sign the papers."	In this organization work is divided into two categories: Projects and Support or maintenance. Even cyclic activities were run as projects. For example a new project to hold the next annual sales meeting begins a couple of weeks after the current year's sales meeting. The team conducts a lessons-learned, begins building a new work charter, analyzes needs, plans events, etc.
Employees have no clear guidelines about how to divide their time because everything is a priority of the day or moment. "This has to be done by noon" is ordered by one manager, while a supervisor can direct "The client presentation is next week and we have not started on it. Let's meet for the next two hours." These situations are the norm rather than the exception.	In fact, even the employees are organized this way so that everyone knows how to devote their time. Support staff focus on administration, break/fix, regular maintenance, etc. Project staff are assigned to work on projects. Not all organizations have enough employees for this but everyone can have set priorities that provide workplace stability.
Tracking budgets, employee allocations, cost/benefit analyses and the real status of projects are impossible.	Tracking costs and adjusting the number of staff to meet an increase in project work or support work happens dynamically and easily because the foundation exists.
While some people used terms like 'dependencies', 'work tasks' and 'authorization', not everyone understood these the same way or accepted authorization of a work order because there is not agreement on these things within the organization. No wonder. If they aren't used regularly and supported the same way, they won't be part of the work culture.	Because formal project management is imbedded, everyone – even the support teams – use terms the same way and talk about minimizing risk or building mitigation strategies if a problem is encountered.

The structured organization took the time and effort to imbed a structure that led to everyone adopting the same vocabulary, expectations, basis of work stability, and in a few years began thinking in terms of minimizing risks, recognizing dependencies and the value of formal authorizations.

The unstructured organization is driven by the next crisis or priority, but even this shifts depending on the manager with the biggest club at that moment. The only common vocabulary and uniform work structure is "do it fast so we can get to the next priority". This organization frustrates each of their clients to some degree and lost a major account after one too many significant problems.

Figure 1: Organization versus Disorganization

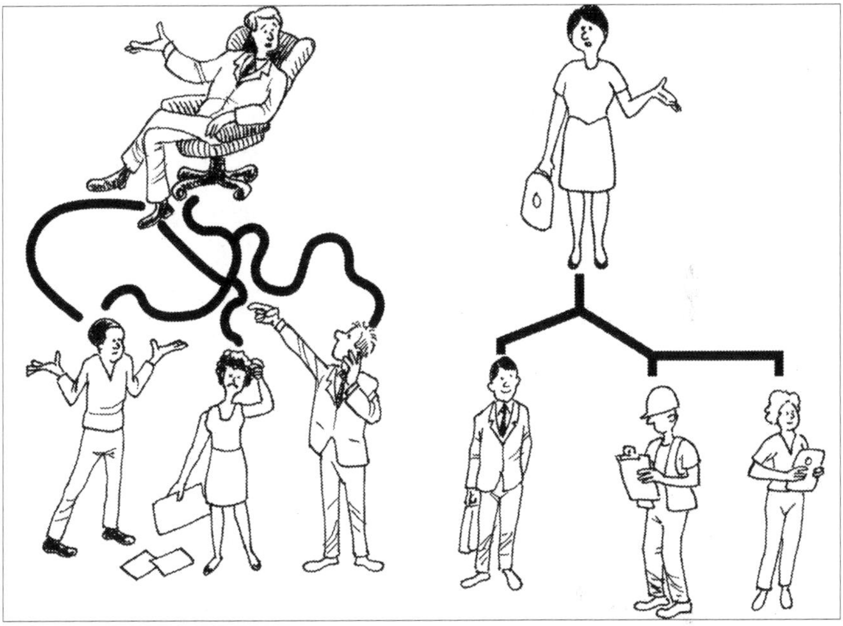

<u>Two Practical Examples</u>

The following descriptions below are to both show that formal processes can be used outside of a formal project structure and that by doing so, organizations will be building a work culture that makes using project management second nature. Here goes…

Planning Knows No Bounds

I've seen several organizations use project management to create focused work, dedicate people to completing the project; all the positive things I could describe about project management. Yet these same organizations don't apply project management principles to control "non-project" work. A real example is the nefarious "reorganization" in which teams, managers and functional units are changed semi-regularly. In one sense a reorganization is like kinetic energy – a lot of potential use that may not exist in its current form. The sentiment is: "Let's see if this new organizational structure unleashes that stored potential."

Yet, I've not seen organizations use a formal structure to plan and manage a reorganization. I may have led a sheltered existence so, I'll merely ask you to evaluate this for your organization:

- Could your company benefit from formal planning of a reorg that identifies the why's, how's, who's, what's and when's of the reorganization?

- Could your company benefit from defining success criteria, defining measurements of the reorg and measurements of success?

- Have reorganizations ever created uncertainty about roles or authority, or created a lot of "this issue just came up so, we need to resolve it quick"? Some colleagues call these "fire drills".

These type of situations can be minimized through careful planning. Planning knows no bounds in the sense that it is not limited to formal projects. Rather, formal projects use planning because it works – regardless of the situation. This is true of all the other project management processes. Risk management, people management, contract management and cost management are inside the overall umbrella of project management because they work and...they know no bounds.

Use Change Management Wherever Change Happens

Change management is used as an example here because it is soooo important to every aspect of completing work. Use a formal change management process, like that presented in Chapter 9, whenever changes occur with any part of your work environment.

Budget cuts are a part of most organizations so, I'll use it as a recognizable example. I've seen many instances in which budgets are cut for entire divisions, work units and even projects, yet they try to do all their work with less. Rather, use change management to evaluate the impact of the budget cuts, i.e. the change. Assess what work can and can't be done, develop a proposal for approval, communicate the impact through the organization, etc. If budgets for projects and programs are cut, their sponsors should lead efforts to analyze, prioritize and present new project proposals.

In my experience, most organizations do this on the fly and the impact of change increases because it is not controlled. So, <u>use change management wherever change happens – even outside of formal projects</u>.

Figure 2: Agreement on What to Cut

"We could cut that deliverable."

Chapter 2: Quick Reference about Projects

The following Key Points are intended to present in short but conversational terms important aspects about project management principles. Note that these are not exhaustive but are sufficient to provide a foundation for you as an executive. Feel free to add your own, discuss with others to develop an exhaustive list for your organization. Also, this information is explained in more detail in my book "Project Management for Executives and Those Who Want to Influence Executives".

Additional references will help complete your project management knowledge, but experience is the best way to learn. I encourage you to actively engage with projects in your organization. Not to micromanage but to see how formal project management adds value. Ask your project managers how you can be involved, partner tightly, then watch the results.

Key points about projects

- <u>Projects are the formal steps, processes, rules, etc. used to complete work.</u>

- <u>Projects have a definite beginning and end</u>; in contrast to continuous production, maintenance or support work.

- <u>Projects have a definite scope</u>, that is, what projects are to deliver is defined, understood similarly by all, discrete and limited, rather than open ended.

- <u>Projects are chartered or formed formally</u> – often by executives or managers, so projects are intentional and should have a champion – like you – who has a vested interest in the work being delivered with quality.

- <u>Projects have specific metrics</u> that can be calculated to show work status, that are used to make decisions about projects as the work is progressing and, can be used to improve how organizations operate.

Key points about roles and teams

- People who work on projects are considered the project team.

- An <u>extended</u> project team includes everyone who has a formal role. This includes people who perform work but probably don't help plan or manage work. Also, this includes executives, sponsors and stakeholders. Some environments don't include sponsors and stakeholders as extended team members. I advocate for this because they are part of escalation processes, can be on change control committees, etc. Make your environment work for you by including sponsors and stakeholder where they can do the most good.

- The <u>core</u> project team are the people who manage the work and who perform the work. This includes roles like team leads, subject matter experts, coordinators, electricians, software coders, etc.

- The project manager is responsible for the project. This means the PM must have the authority needed to ensure the core team can complete the work. It also means the PM must be supported by a project champion; this should be an executive.

- Project teams must have the autonomy to operate without interference. The project charter provides the team with their operational mission and objectives. Keep them free from interference so they can complete the mission.

Key points about managing projects

- Project managers manage projects with three tools: Plans, Metrics and Authority.
    - ○ Plans which are the activities and rules used to manage parts of the work. For example, the Scope Management plan specifies how to identify scope and protect it throughout the project.
    - ○ Metrics regarding cost, time and scope. Cost metrics reflect actual costs to the current point in the project and estimated total costs to complete the project. Both are compared to the original estimated cost. Time metrics are similar to costs but reflect actual schedule to the current point in the project and estimated future dates compared to the original scheduled date. Scope metrics reflect status of deliverables, e.g. the percent complete of deliverables. Combined, these metrics can be used to make many decisions, like cutting some scope in order to complete others. These three components are related and presented in the 'Triple Constraint' diagram.
    - ○ Authority to control the work should come with the territory. Imagine a Western movie in which the Lawman can't carry a gun, doesn't have a jail and, the deputies don't help him. Project managers need to have the authority that matches their responsibility and accountability to deliver value by completing the work. More on this later.
- Managing projects is distinctly different from managing how people complete the work. Project managers do not necessarily manage software algorithm development, lab technician protocol or reverse-treatment experiments. Understandably within small organizations project managers may be required to become involved in more details than in larger organizations. But as a general rule,

in order to enforce the project plan the PM should not be distracted by details of doing the work.

- <u>Changes to the work must be analyzed and planned</u> or they can be huge sources of project conflicts.

- <u>The most significant contributors to project success are</u>:
    - o Defining the work.
    - o Developing and following plans to complete the work.
    - o Having a project manager with authority and a champion, like you, actively partnering with the PM to support the project.
    - o Controlling change.

Architecture of successful projects

The foundations and dependencies of architecting successful projects is shown in the diagram below. Initiation and Defining the work form the foundation. Planning how to manage the work forms the control panel. Executing the work builds deliverables. Work things out with Monitoring and Controlling. Close out so you can turn off the lights.

Figure 3: Foundational Steps of Successful Projects

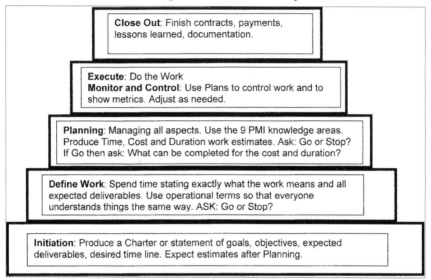

Close Out: Finish contracts, payments, lessons learned, documentation.

Execute: Do the Work
Monitor and Control: Use Plans to control work and to show metrics. Adjust as needed.

Planning: Managing all aspects. Use the 9 PMI knowledge areas. Produce Time, Cost and Duration work estimates. Ask: Go or Stop? If Go then ask: What can be completed for the cost and duration?

Define Work: Spend time stating exactly what the work means and all expected deliverables. Use operational terms so that everyone understands things the same way. ASK: Go or Stop?

Initiation: Produce a Charter or statement of goals, objectives, expected deliverables, desired time line. Expect estimates after Planning.

The triple constraint, iron triangle and three-legged stool

Figure 4: Triple Constraint Iron Triangle and Three-Legged Stool

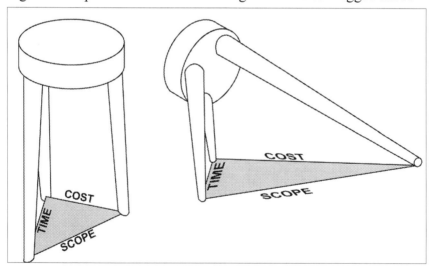

Chapter 3: Instilling Foundations in Your Organization

Overview

I'm not a huge slogan type of person – really! However, slogans help reinforce concepts, serve as metaphors and mental pictures. They are excellent at instilling foundations in your organization. Several slogans are presented in this chapter, as well as activities that will help instill foundations for a success-oriented work environment.

Slogans and handles are great ways to encapsulate key success factors as phrases and mental pictures that help people see what successful projects look like. Certainly these are not exhaustive and not all are original "Houseworthisms".

Development Exercise: A great exercise is to write the handles and slogans on slips of paper, distribute them to people for discussion and their descriptions. Next bring them back together to compare their descriptions with the description presented here.

The exercise surfaces biases, pain points, "if we could only do this" and "yeah, like that will work in this place" sentiments. Be prepared for these. I recommend conducting these exercises with upper management first to build support, then talking to unit managers and teams next.

Handles

Most of us know what slogans are but in case you aren't familiar with 'handles', they are short statements that people can visualize, grasp and use. To say "That sounds like a Dilbert" is to state a handle, i.e. use the concepts of problems in the corporate workplace portrayed in the Dilbert cartoons.

Other handles include the two statements from the Introduction, i.e. <u>Insanity</u> and that other term you assigned to "Doing the same things repeatedly knowing you'll have problems". Others:

- Like trying to hold a wet bar of soap in the shower. Squeeze too hard and it squirts out. Hold too loose and it slips out. Need to apply just the right pressure or firmness.
- Projects are about adding value.
- Are we adding value or reducing value?

Project Management Slogans

Plan the Work, then Work the Plan

Explanation: You've probably heard the Lewis Carroll saying that "If you don't know where you are going, any road will get you there." In project management terms, all work should have a plan to accomplish it. The plan includes how to make sure the work is defined, i.e. everyone working on it understands the work in the same way. The plan includes how to measure success, how to communicate the work status to people who need to know, how to know who needs to know, etc. If the work is planned for all the factors and contingencies, it can be executed, communicated and delivered without many difficulties. So, the level of planning should match the planning required for the type of work. The planning itself can take weeks, or months. Another key point is that the work should not begin until the plan is complete enough to guide the work.

Get the Right People, at the Right Time, to do the Right Work, in the Right Way

Explanation: I think this slogan along with "Plan the work, then work the plan", encapsulate the essential features of formal project management. This slogan drips experience and reality. Think about the components:

- The "right people" are only known if the work is defined well enough to know the skills and numbers of the work force needed to complete it.

- The "right time" implies work sequences. Some work is dependent on other work. Also, that the amount of work time needed can be estimated and calculated so that people have sufficient time to complete it.

- The "right work" implies that the work is defined to a sufficient degree to know who, how and when it can be completed.

- The "right way" implies that the work has been analyzed, is planned and will proceed intelligently.

Work to Know, then Work What You Know

Explanation: Completing work is often a series of discoveries. Some are small while others are large. Formal project management follows the premise that what is not known can't be planned, scheduled or completed. So, this slogan emphasizes resolving what is not known so that it can be worked. Assumptions should be avoided and replaced with knowledge.

Work Smart First, Hard Second

I've seen the work culture in organizations emphasize being busy as in busy-ness rather than effectiveness. Project management, in essence, emphasizes working smart rather than just working. I like to say that if we work smart first we won't need to work as hard later. Even so, the ethic that busy-ness equates to meaningful work is tough to change in most work environments. Changing this requires at least these two factors: First, analyzing whether people are busy working smart or busy fixing issues because they have not been encouraged to work smart. Second, a cultural acceptance that thinking, planning, analyzing and documenting, etc. is real work. This is the "thought that precedes action" and the "ounce of prevention" rather than a "pound of cure". As an executive you are in an excellent position to influence this change. A corollary to this slogan is presented next.

Just Because People Are Busy Does Not Mean They Are Productive

Explanation: Without an adequate plan to execute work, a lot of people can do work that is useless: Developing charts, crunching numbers, designing electrical schematics, writing status reports, developing software code, etc. All of which could be irrelevant if the work is not defined adequately, if work changes or, if the plan changes based upon the work. I've seen this happen far too often. In fact, I continue to see it. As an executive, you need to be acutely sensitive to wasted time equaling wasted money. Project management begins with defining the work, then planning the work, ensuring that the people assigned to do the work are productive.

Figure 5: Wasted Time = Wasted Money

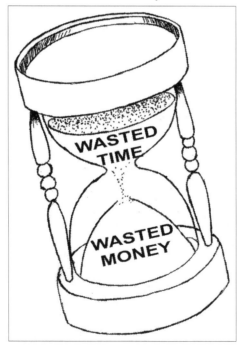

The Immediate Always Delays the Inevitable

Explanation: Even if the work is defined and planned, its status within an organization is always potentially threatened by other work that has higher priority. This higher priority work is often presented as an immediate issue. People are told to stop what they are doing to focus on something else. Now I understand that sometimes the immediate is higher priority. Consequently, strategic, longer-term work such as project work is delayed because of the immediate crisis. Formal project management develops work schedules then maintains metrics based on the schedules. The metrics are not to point fingers, level guilt, or to praise people for completing work early. The metrics are status indicators, i.e. how does reality match earlier expectations? The best way to ensure that your work stays as close to schedule as possible is to assess the relative priority of project work and the immediate crisis.

How **Bad** Do You **Want** It, Because that is How **Bad** You'll **Get** It

Explanation: Rushed work is usually substandard, defective and cost more to fix than doing the work the right way in the first place. I was told this slogan years ago by a test coordinator in response to my complaints about sponsors wanting to maintain a schedule by streamlining testing. He suggested I ask them, how bad they wanted it because that is how bad they were likely to get it, if they shortened testing. Of course the initial clause is about emotion while the ultimate clause is about quality. Formal project management includes mechanisms to check emotion so that rationality is maintained and quality can be delivered.

Figure 6: How Bad do you Want It

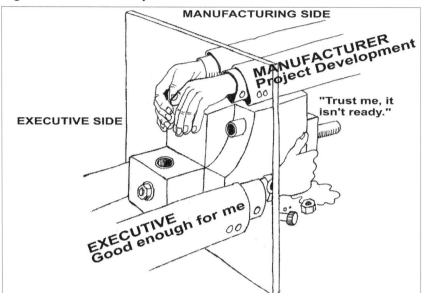

Play the Ball, Don't Let the Ball Play You

I use this slogan mostly in reference to methodologies and schedules. Think in terms of baseball, basketball, softball, soccer, tennis, golf – just about any ball sport. Balls are tools and objects to accomplish the goals of the sport. Athletes are more effective when they actively judge the ball's speed, rotation, angle, then adjust to make the ball do what they want: fall into their glove, hit it in the racquet's sweet spot or loft a great pass.

Project methodologies and schedules, like a ball, are tools and objects used to help control and manage work. They should be adjusted based on unique features of the work. Schedules are often adjusted based on actual circumstances and need. One methodology does not fit all types of projects, so adjust. Use these tools but don't let the tools rule you. This does not mean to abandon a methodology phase or let the schedule slip. It does mean that the project team is in control, not the tool.

How to apply: Activities to instill foundations

As you read these activity ideas, you'll probably develop your own. I encourage you to brainstorm and collaborate with colleagues about other slogans and activities and ways to instill them as part of your organizational foundations.

Executive statements

Formal statements about the role of project management, the organization's commitment to it and expectations for everyone to support it are crucial. Executives should use slogans that are adopted by your organization. This sets the standard for everyone to be held accountable, for everyone to feel free to use slogans, for everyone to understand that adding value is what a project management work environment is all about.

Consider during meetings stating your slogans, the role of project management, metrics that show progress, and real examples. Include executive statements during kick-off of organization education activities, active exercises and working sessions. Doing this really reinforces commitment from the highest level. Not doing this raises the prospect that at some point, when compromises are made or policies are not enforced, that statements about project management are nice sound bites but it is not really supported.

Unit or team exercises and discussions

Build slogans into unit or team activities. These are great opportunities to surface pros and cons – and cons exist in every environment. Management can field questions, explain how they would support employees who follow process and challenge employees when process is not followed. It is also a great opportunity to pose scenarios and clarify the amount of control needed to protect work so that it adds value. Project controls will be addressed more fully in subsequent chapters.

Ask employees to develop their own slogans and share situations that reinforce the principles. Team members will learn the various steps in managing work as projects, so several small groups can be assigned to report on each of the steps, knowledge areas, sample metrics and, how to avoid unnecessary process.

Organization-wide exercises

Trivia contests, board games, interdepartmental workshops, etc. are great ethic building activities. Your organization may be large enough to develop some fairly sophisticated exercises, props, game boards, maybe even software games. Your organization may be small so that flash card exercises are all your budget can afford. No matter what you can afford, organization-wide exercises demonstrate commitment, promote common terms and vocabulary and, add value you'll receive back in abundance by the synergy they generate.

Chapter 4:   Steps of all work – in or out of a project framework

Formal or informal, all work goes through the same steps

The final foundation component I've found in organizations is understanding that that all work goes through the same steps, whether within structured processes or informal, ad-hoc processes.

All work goes through these major steps:

- Envisioning or initiating = Initial idea or need to "let's do it".

- Planning = How completing the work should be conducted.

- Analysis = Determining the details, discovery steps, literature reviews. Sometimes this leads to more planning and better planning supports better analysis…until you are ready to prepare.

- Preparation = Creating the environment, developing the skills, getting the equipment, etc.

- Execution, building, or doing = Plumbing fluid lines, anchoring braces, writing software code, creating blueprints.

- Test or checking = Making sure it works the way it should.

- Cleaning up = Returning equipment, final approvals, paying holdbacks, etc.

You may want to include some additional steps and you would be right if you said that each of these steps includes other steps. Again, these are the major steps. Also, if you are familiar with the Project Management Institute's 5 work phases, you'll notice that mine don't match exactly. And that is OK too. My main point in presenting these phases is to provide a framework for you. Add or subtract phases for the nature of your work. Whether you use these major steps or create your own, they should progress a planned, purposeful and organized sequence.

And that makes sense. Most people can form loose mental plans and sequence through them. With enough experience people can refine these mental plans and become quite skilled navigating sequential processes and completing work without formal, written plans, risk management criteria, or quality measurements. But two substantial differences exist between projects that can be mastered this way and most business projects: Complexity and professionalism.

Most business projects have an inherent level of complexity and have at risk non-trivial monetary consequences. These deserve more than loose mental plans.

Think about it. Have you ever been part way through a project at work or at home then realized, "I can't go much further unless I take care of something I did not realize earlier." Whether you are cooking Thanksgiving dinner for a large group or making major home improvements, you've probably experienced the contrast between those things you planned well and those you did not. A saying among my Do-It-Yourself friends is, "every job requires at least three trips to the home improvement store and leaves you with extra parts you hope can be used in the next decade." But then, I'm not a construction or automotive professional. When I do use professionals, I always ask them questions about their planning, sequencing, do I need to move furniture or lay down tarps to prepare for them, etc. I expect that they will have the right tools and equipment so they won't take several trips for parts.

Comparing work steps within and without a project management work environment

Here is a short exercise contrasting the value of project management versus not using project management, considering that the major work steps are the same either way.

Table 2: Characteristics of Work Within & Without Project Management

Characteristics of work within a Project Management Environment	Characteristics of work without a Project Management Environment
Formalized	Informal
Measurements to guide work	Anecdotal information, memory or hunches
Sequential and purposeful	Logical with some randomness
Structured and complete	Unstructured and piecemeal or iterative
Purposeful discovery	Chance discovery
Controlled, particularly for gathering information, documenting, delivering reports to others.	Uncontrolled or minimal control. This often leads to poor quality, rework, hecticness, on the spot "We can do that by then" statements.
Anticipating risks and planning for them	Dealing with risks as they happen

Compare characteristics between the left-side and right-side.

A project management work environment ensures the features on the left side. Many potential risks are inherent on the right side. Metrics to manage and make decisions are inherent on the left side while hunches are about the best measurements available on the right side.

One of my teams was ready to deploy dozens of improvements to a software application. If everything worked right – and testing indicated they should work – users all across the U.S. would have a lot of new functionality. However, deployment presents its own challenges. Because my team could not predict what would happen, we could have let the deployment proceed without any additional planning. I thought that was too risky so, I told them: "Look, even though we can't predict what will happen, you are the software experts so develop your list of the top 10 problems that can happen and develop mitigation steps to handle these. Also, think of the top 10 things users might do if they try to skip the navigation menus or wizards. Develop mitigation steps for these. Because we were proactive, the team actually had ready-to-use steps when these situations occurred. Even though not all the situations occurred, the team operated professionally and was ready for a reasonable set of situations.

Conclusion: Using formal project management principles is well worth the time and effort.

Conclusion: Your organization will spend at least as much time to complete work without using project management principles as with them. Most likely more time will be needed without them.

To those who say planning takes too long and besides, the workers already know what to do:

- They are working from the right side of the table.

- Say "OK! Show how all the left-side factors are managed without planning". If they can, Great!. If not, they use a self reflecting discovery process to show their premise is not accurate.

- Costs of rework, errors, defects, etc. grow exponentially throughout the work and into the final product. I have developed a tool, presented in Chapter 9, that can be used to quantify the value of catching errors.

Think of formal project processes as a time exchange

I like to explain that the time needed to complete work using rigorous, structured processes and rules, i.e. project management principles, should be considered <u>a time exchange between spending the time to do the work right versus the time needed to fix things as you go and after finishing</u>.

Figure 7: Time Exchange

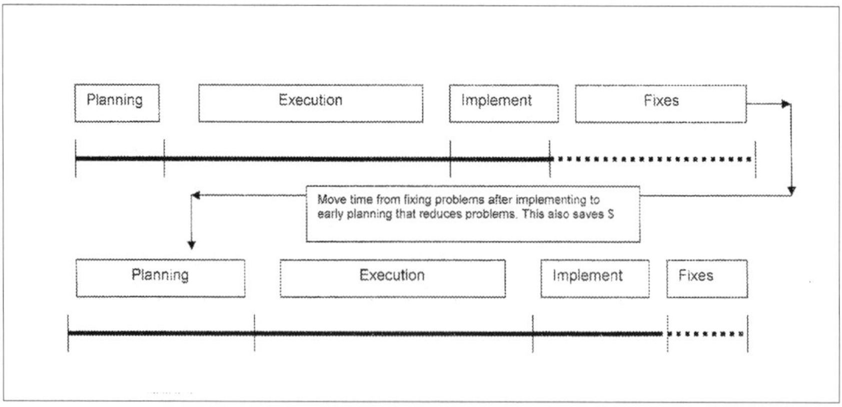

Even if the amount of time were exactly the same, formalizing work processes results in less frustration and superior control than working ad-hoc. Fortunately, in most cases you'll spend less time also.

Remember the slogans "Just because people are busy doesn't mean they are productive" and "How **bad** do you want it because that is how **bad** you'll get it." Just because some products have been delivered doesn't mean the products work right, will last through the warranty period, etc. If additional work is needed to fix what could have been prevented earlier, then that work effort really is not over. Oh, <u>most organizations don't have ways of measuring this extra work</u>, but it is real and should be recognized.

Think in terms of end-to-end work effort

The long tail of fixing problems is why I consider this content a foundation for improving your project management work environment. <u>Organizations need to think of work efforts in terms of end-to-end impacts</u>. Remember project management is about completing work that adds value. The end-to-end cost assessment must be considered in the total value-added equation. If your organization measured costs throughout the long tail of fixing problems then the cost-benefit ratio could decrease significantly. The costs inherent in rigorous planning, analysis, preparation that lead to effective execution and testing that result in quality products with few defects is usually far less costly than ad-hoc work with a long tail of fixes.

Think of your organization's operational maturity

Finally, to add a bit of humor and emphasis I'm often reminded of things my parents tried to drill out of me by the time I was through junior high school. I've done the same with my kids. My two sons were very active and loved to play outside. When I heard a loud bang against the house, car or windows, I'd usually find a football, soccer ball, golf ball, Frisbee, etc. was involved. Trying to understand their adolescent frame of mind, I'd ask "how did that happen?" The usual reply was that they "did not think they would" hit the house or car. This was the teachable moment I could use to help them mature their thought processes. I'd ask "Well, <u>what did you do to make sure you couldn't hit the house?</u>" The usual answer was "Nothing." "Well then, next time think about what could happen, then do things to make sure it does not happen." was my lesson message. This worked well and fortunately I never replaced a window.

Figure 8: Make Sure Something Bad Can't Happen

How often in work environments do you find people still working at what I call a "junior high logic level." If something bad happens will the rationale be because people did not think it could happen so they did not ensure it could not happen? This is a major difference between using and not using rigor, structured processes and rules to manage work, i.e. project management principles. You may think that calling this "junior high logic" is demeaning and too inferior a reference. You may have a point, but that is exactly why I use that phrase. Professionals should operate better than this and such a phrase is effective at getting professionals to raise their level of planning and execution.

Here is a simple example from information technology, but it can apply in any industry. One project team was fond of pointing out problems caused by a contractor and the fact that "no other project manager has held them accountable." I was new to the team and the contractor so I had an opportunity to build credibility with the team by holding the contractor accountable. Part way through testing my team encountered a problem with the databases which several team members blamed on the contractor. I told them that before we targeted accusations they needed to find the root cause so I could take it to the contractor. This is an example of "work to know, then work what you know." Well, turned out that one of my team members was the culprit. He had not made updates in one of the three databases that had to be in synch. So, I asked him if he used a written and physical checklist or a mental checklist whenever he needed to make updates. "Mental checklist" he told me. My reply was "Let's use a written checklist so we don't lose half a day troubleshooting a problem because you assumed this was caused by the contractor." He agreed.

No matter how well people think they know their work, professionals should do things – like develop checklists – to ensure that bad things can't happen. Again, while nothing is fool proof, the effort is needed.

How to apply

1. Conduct discussions about steps that all work goes through, whether formalized or not.
   a. First with management so they have first hand experience to use during employee discussions.
   b. Second with employees.

2. Note the types of issues both management and employees describe. These will be themes that can be addressed as your organization implements their project management work environment.
3. Conduct an exercise with employees using the "Characteristics of Work Within / Without Project Management" chart.
    a. Ask them to contrast the left and right columns.
    b. Ask them about how to balance the level of planning and rigor needed for the left side in order to avoid the right side.
4. Make your own list of steps work goes through, principles, real examples, etc. from both management and employees. You'll want to address these as you build your formal work environment.

Section 2: Form and Function

I am a firm believer that the main task of management is to create the environment in which employees want to work, are motivated to work and gain self-worth through what they do. Creating and improving a project management work environment fits within this task of management. Up to this point of the book only the work culture foundation has been provided. This section adds elements employees can see, feel, use and reference as tools and guiding principles.

The content in Chapters 5, 6 and 7 are nonsequential. You can read them in just about any order, but they are dependent and reinforce each other in many respects. Chapter 5 presents facilitating processes, which are formal ways people can work efficiently and with quality. For example, conducting efficient meetings with set agendas can save hours each day or week, allowing employees to be more productive. Chapter 6 describes a great way to get your team to identify and understand the work steps needed to complete a project with sufficient detail. I call this a Work Breakdown Discovery process. Its results have been proven through use in many organizations. Chapter 7 presents metrics, which are often overlooked in organizations. How will you know if your goals are achieved? How will you learn from projects? Many organizations want to use project management to improve operations, but they don't take the time to plan metrics to guide decisions about their work or their organization.

These chapters provide the form and function for the living, active organism that your organization will recognize as their project management work environment.

Chapter 5:   Facilitating processes

How they can add value

Ever sit through meetings that seem to go from 10:00 to infinity? Do people in your organization ever say that making a decision will take weeks because of the difficulty of getting everyone together? Do internal politics, turf battles and differing perspectives of company/ unit direction reduce the chances for developing consensus about a topic?

Have you ever seen a topic clarified so that people and units with divergent views come to an agreement? It really is a neat accomplishment. Do you have examples where a third party was able to mediate an issue so that disagreeing parties felt their side was improved? How about resolving a complex decision in a few hours rather than several weeks?

Think of facilitating processes as

- Catalysts that help people work efficiently.
- Structured thinking that helps people focus on essential elements without being distracted by nonessential elements.
- Formal steps to prepare for meetings and to alleviate potential conflicts so that work remains task focused.

As a reference point, some of this content is presented in the book "Project Management for Executives and Those Who Want to Influence Executives" in the chapter "Soft Skills Rule". The purpose of this book is more amenable to presenting more detail about how to use facilitated processes. I encourage you to search the internet for more examples and related facilitated processes.

Integrate facilitation formally into your organization

Everyone in your organization can learn facilitation principles and techniques to use during everyday work. I recommend that some become facilitation specialists. One example of a specialist role from software development is the role of the Modeler, who leads people through discussions that result in very effective automated system architectures and designs. Learning and using facilitation techniques is usually self-reinforcing, that is, the more techniques are used and the value made evident, the more people use them and expect others to use them. For example: "I like your meetings, Wendy, because they only last as long as needed and we actually make progress. Howard's meetings are sheer drudgery and we end up talking about the same things for weeks."

Examples of facilitating processes:

- Structured Meetings with rules and set agendas
- Modeling and work flow
- Situation Analysis
- Topic definition
- Decision Making
- Problem Solving
- Risk and Opportunity Analysis
- Mediation
- Brainstorming
- Escalation steps
- Work Breakdown Structure discovery

I like to say that for most facilitating processes there is nothing new under the sun. Success is a matter of structuring what is under the sun in a planned and purposeful way. To this end, some key success factors will be needed, such as:

- <u>Delegated authority to one leader</u> who has a set mission. This mission may be to lead an effective meeting, conduct modeling or help a team use the Isikawa technique to figure out why compressor seals are failing.

- <u>Structured processes</u> used to accomplish a specific mission. Decision making processes are different than brainstorming, but both are structured.

- <u>Commitment by participants to the mission</u> rather than not caring to participate or commitment to their own agendas.

- <u>Documentation of discussion and results</u> so that no one can say "I don't remember it that way."

By the way, I use the terms facilitated sessions and working sessions synonymously here. I know that facilitation purists distinguish between these, but we don't need to be that particular for showing how these contribute to creating and improving a project management work environment.

Here are some rules I've adopted that ensure a stable working environment during facilitated sessions and meetings. I recommend they be published, posted, distributed and explained prior to each meeting or session and reinforced during sessions. Feel free to add your own.

1. The session leader or team leader controls the session / meeting.

2. Begin on time and end on time. This includes returning from breaks.

3. Present the agenda then work the agenda. If no agenda then don't meet.

4. Come prepared with facts, notes, metrics, etc. Do your homework so the session can be successful.

5. Focus on the agenda topic(s) for the organization. Leave your personal agenda at the door. Note: Some facilitators/leaders actually have "baggage boxes", like a shoe box with a slit cut in the top so attendees can write their personal agendas or "baggage" they may bring to the session, then drop this in the box. The box is taken out of the room to symbolize that personal agendas

aren't part of the solution. This may or may not work in your organization.

6. Everyone has an equal voice.

7. Respect others and they'll respect you.

8. One conversation at a time. No side conversations.

9. Let others finish speaking before you speak – don't interrupt.

10. The leader or recorder will record <u>only</u> what is said or decided. If they interpret or restate themes, they will ask for agreement that it represents what is meant.

11. Contribute to the process within the sessions, don't backdoor decisions outside of the sessions.

12. Observers, rather than participants, are allowed but they cannot speak or contribute. This prevents someone with positional power from attending and skewing the agenda away from the active participants.

The absolute best facilitator I've ever seen is a small, petite woman with a soft voice. Deb knows how to establish session rules and agendas. She interviews many participants prior to the sessions so that she understands the background of topics, internal politics, personal agendas, etc. She explains that she has no vested interest in the session agenda. In fact, she seldom has subject matter expertise. Her only goal is to help participants achieve the goals of the session. She posts her 'rules' and takes the first five minutes to review and explain them. Then she proceeds to focus on the topic and control the session with many light touches. Her strongest approach is to turn lights off and on to disrupt those who are disruptive in order to reestablish her control as the session leader. She is able to turn a stalemate – not every session follows script – into a success with phrases like: "Well, I'm hearing you say that several unresolved topics need to be addressed before we can accomplish the purpose of this meeting. I'll send our notes to the session sponsor and let them pursue these topics. We can hold another session to resolve these topics or meet on this agenda again after these topics are resolved."

The value of definitions

Figure 9: Define the Topic

Define, so everyone understands

Every group activity depends absolutely on everyone understanding topics, terms, etc. the same way. I recommend strongly that everyone in your organization ensure this as the first step in any topic discussion and working session.

Consider a topic as seemingly simple as "Control Disruptions in the

Work Environment". Asking participants what this means may seem to be unnecessary until you hear perspectives.

"The computing network crashes unexpectedly too often. This has to be fixed. The work environment is too fragile."

"I thought this was about all the consultants who come in to tell us what to do. We have experts in our environment too. Consultants are too disruptive."

"Too many loud conversations that interrupt my thoughts and hurt phone conversations. The work environment has to be controlled better."

The sponsor may have created the topic phrase as a neutral statement that would not create undue reactions before the session but as these comments indicate, it is too vague. Perhaps all of these topics need to be addressed, but each topic is so unrelated to the other that more than likely only one is the real session topic.

Define the topic and any terms by asking clarifying questions like:

- Can you provide some examples?
- How would resolving this make a difference?
- Are other factors involved or related?
- How would you state the problem or issue?

Often the simple exercise of defining the topic helps others understand perspectives, fills in gaps and helps people begin to think of options to contribute later during working sessions. While Topic Definition can be a legitimate session of its own, this usually is the initial step of other facilitated working sessions.

Modeling and work flow

Modeling is actually quite straightforward. Use diagrams and lines or arrows to indicate how work begins, flows and completes. Many industries use specific symbols to represent input, output, storage, circuits, etc. Think of modeling and work flow diagrams as the work flow equivalent of electrical or architectural schematics and blueprints. Modeling provides a visual representation of reality. This visual representation allows fairly easy viewing of relationships, bottlenecks, decision points, facilitating processes as well as rogue elements.

While I have used modeling frequently, one example is illustrative. I became manager of a support team that was so busy I needed to hire three more staff soon after becoming manager. Problem was that no documentation existed to train the new staff and the team said they were too busy to even train new staff. Within two weeks I learned that so many unique conditions existed that I had to glean the knowledge from the existing team before one of them won the lottery and took all that knowledge with them. They reluctantly agreed to spend two hours a day modeling their processes until complete – which took two weeks. But the result was visual flow processes with if-then conditions, daily and weekly sequences and deadlines for approvals and reports, etc. These provided:

- Step by step guides for everyone to follow.
- Solid documentation to update as needed so that it remained current.
- Training for new employees. Particularly cross training so team members could perform someone else's role when another team member was out of the office.
- Quality control and evaluation criteria.
- Stability and mental comfort.

The mood of the team changed dramatically from hectic and anxious to calm and confident.

Here is a short model example:

Figure 10: Work Flow Modeling Sample

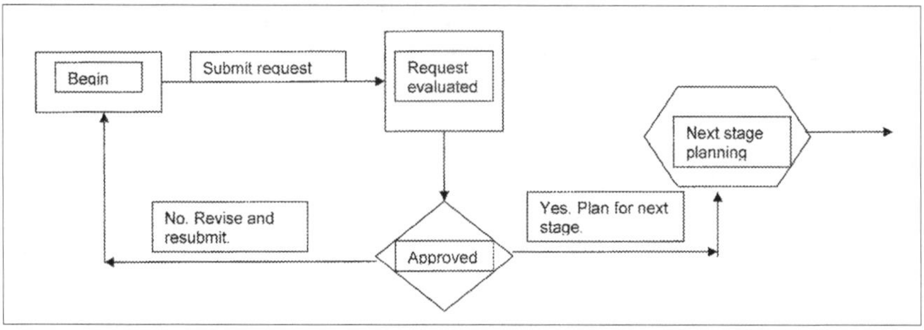

Modeling in your organization should be much more detailed, but you get the idea.

Problem Solving following the Ishikawa or Fishbone Diagramming Method

From Vanderbilt University: http://mot.vuse.vanderbilt.edu/mt322/Ishikawa.htm

Definition: A graphic tool used to explore and display opinion about sources of variation in a process. (Also called a Cause-and-Effect or Fishbone Diagram.)

Purpose: To arrive at a few key sources that contribute most significantly to the problem being examined. These sources are then targeted for improvement. The diagram also illustrates the relationships among the wide variety of possible contributors to the effect.

The figure below shows a simple Ishikawa diagram. Note that this tool is referred to by several different names: Ishikawa diagram, Cause-and-Effect diagram, Fishbone diagram, and Root Cause Analysis. The first name is after the inventor of the tool, Kaoru Ishikawa (1969) who first used the technique in the 1960s.

The basic concept in the Cause-and-Effect diagram is that the name of a basic problem of interest is entered at the right of the diagram at the end of the main "bone". The main possible causes of the problem (the effect) are drawn as bones off of the main backbone. The "Four-M" categories are typically used as a starting point:

"Materials", "Machines", "Manpower", and "Methods". Different names can be chosen to suit the problem at hand, or these general categories can be revised. The key is to have three to six main categories that encompass all possible influences. Brainstorming is typically done to add possible causes to the main "bones" and more specific causes to the "bones" on the main "bones". This subdivision into ever increasing specificity continues as long as the problem areas can be further subdivided. The practical maximum depth of this tree is usually about four or five levels. When the fishbone is complete, one has a rather complete picture of all the possibilities about what could be the root cause for the designated problem.

The Cause-and-Effect diagram can be used by individuals or teams; probably most effectively by a group. A typical utilization is the drawing of a diagram on a blackboard by a team leader who first presents the main problem and asks for assistance from the group to determine the main causes which are subsequently drawn on the board as the main bones of the diagram. The team assists by making suggestions and, eventually, the entire cause and effect diagram is filled out. Once the entire fishbone is complete, team discussion takes place to decide what are the most likely root causes of the problem. These causes are circled to indicate items that should be acted upon, and the use of the tool is complete.

The Ishikawa diagram, like most quality tools, is a visualization and knowledge organization tool. Simply collecting the ideas of a group in a systematic way facilitates the understanding and ultimate diagnosis of the problem.

Here is a fairly realistic completed diagram I found at www.siliconefareast.com.

Of course the problem statement, main bones and sub-bones will be unique to your organization. Not only is this a great tool for PMs and team leads but it is also a great reference document to appreciate subject matter and situations your staff encounters and must resolve within projects.

Figure 11: Ishikawa or Fishbone Diagram

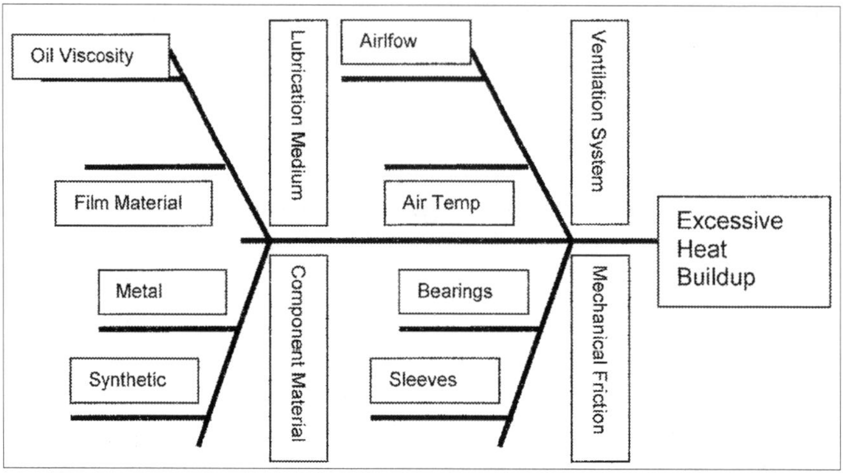

Think of this diagramming technique as a way to visually organize topical information then trace related topics. Well, in addition to problem solving this technique is also a great way to organize planning topics. Here is an example.

Figure 12: Ishikawa for Planning

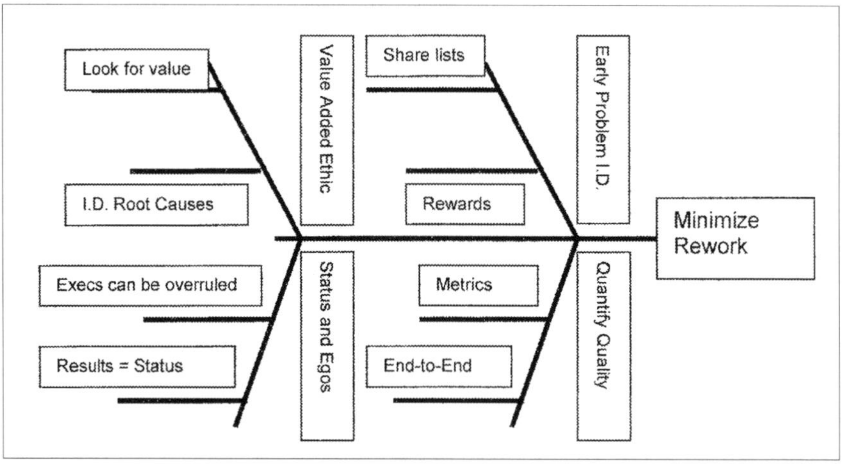

Structured Decision Analysis

I have used the Kepner-Tregoe decision analysis technique successfully in a variety of situations. It is not the only decision analysis technique and again, I like to say that "There is nothing new under the sun" with it. Its value is the structure and rigor that provide empirical evaluation. Note that I do not say objective or unbiased evaluation because this is not possible. However, two key features that all parties involved need to agree are:

- The categories of 'Must Have' and 'Nice to Have'.
- The rankings and values of the options to be decided.

Here is a spreadsheet example. A blank template is in the appendix. The objective is to select which of Options A, B or C best meet the Objectives, which are classified as Musts or Wants. <u>Must objectives</u> are not ranked or rated because they are essential. Consequently, they are used to exclude options that do not meet them. <u>Want objectives</u> are assigned a value from 1-10 to reflect a relative value. How complete each option satisfies each want is assigned as the <u>Want Rating</u> from 1-10. <u>Scores equal the Want Value X the Want Rating</u> for each Option. Scores are totaled at the bottom. In this example, a perfect score is 350. Option A scores 274, Option B scores 203 while Option C scores 173. Then a risk and opportunity analysis is performed based on other criteria. Could be how much maintenance the option requires, the relative inexperience of the option within the organization, etc. Option A is a low risk. Option B does not satisfy two Musts so, it is excluded. Option A meets the objectives best and Option C is selected as the alternate vendor.

Table 3: Decision Analysis Matrix Sample

Decision Analysis Matrix Sample

Decision Objective: Select a new LOB application

Key: Precise statement. No ambiguity. Objective evaluation and selection

Objectives	Must or Want	Want Value (1-10)	Option A			Option B			Option C		
	Must		Meet Must	Want Rating (1-10)	Want Percent (score X Want value)	Meet Must	Want Rating (1-10)	Want Percent (score X Want value)	Meet Must	Want Rating (1-10)	Want Percent (score X Want value)
Browser based	Must		Yes		0	No		0	Y		0
Compatible w/existing database	Must		Yes		0	Y		0	Y		0
Uses same database	Want	5	Yes	10	5 * 10 = 50	Y	0	5 * 0 = 0	Y	5	5 * 5 = 25
Individual letter generation	Must		Yes		0	Y		0	Y		0
Batch/mass letter generation	Must		Yes		0	Y		0	Y		0
Configurable calculation engine	Want	9	Yes	6	9 * 6 = 54		7	9 * 7 =63		0	9 * 0 = 0
Standard actuarial formulas	Must		Yes		0	Y		0	Y		0
Create custom actuarial formulas	Want	8		5	8 * 5 = 40		10	8*10 = 80		7	8 * 7 = 56
Integrates w/time reporting system	Want	6		10	6 * 10 = 60		10	6 *10 = 60		6	6 * 6 = 36
MS-Windows Server system	Must		Yes		0	Y		0	Y		0
Security via Active Directory	Want	7		10	7 * 10 = 70	Y	0	7 * 0 = 0		8	7 * 8 = 56
Security configurable by staff role	Must		Yes		0	No		0	Y		0
Score		350			274			203			173
Result	Want	Perfect Score			High Score			Eliminate: Two musts not met			Second
Conduct Risk/ Opportunity analysis					Low risk Preferred vendor						Moderate risk Alternate vendor
Final Decision											

Again, I have seen this used successfully to analyze complex situations to determine decisions. The structure builds consensus and diffuses personal influences. The duration depends on several factors, from a few hours in one session to multiple sessions over a couple of weeks. Usually the longer duration is due to the need for more information, fact finding, consulting with other related areas, etc.

All facilitated processes should be preceded by as much fact finding as possible. This includes

- Subject matter specifics
- Participant relationships, i.e. cliques, strains
- Organization strategic factors like 3-5 year plans

Kaizen, Obeya and Hansei

Kaizen means "continuous improvement. Obeya means literally "Big Room". Hansei means "reflection" as in review, examine and improve. Many work environments use these as part of adding value. Like so many other ways to add value, the real key is a commitment to use them so, before I provide more detail I want to emphasize that purposeful planning and activities need to be developed or these will be just another set of nice words that could but are not providing value.

Again, many resources are available so search the internet to learn more detail and for sources that fit your type of organization. The Lean Enterprise Institute is an excellent source: www.lean.org.

Another source I like is Superfactory: factory strategies group LLC: http://www.superfactory.com/topics/

Conduct your own internet search. You'll find a wealth of resources on these topics and many others.

Oh, one word of balance. Just because these are terms that denote process improvement and quality orientation, does not mean that they don't involve time, effort and purposeful management. They do not work automatically or by osmosis, but like my admonitions throughout the book, only by focusing on how to add value to your organization with planning and purpose.

Kaizen

Continuous improvement is in many ways analogous to ongoing lessons learned. The ISO 9000 has formalized this into its processes. Often improvement is the result of improving small processes so, don't look just for large improvements. In fact, even large improvements should be decomposed into smaller units with plans and measurements to track results. This may be a way to save one side step by an assembler that is repeated hundreds of times per day or using convex mirrors to see around corners and prevent collisions. Kaizan also fits the emphasis that improvement is everyone's duty and right. Sometimes a forklift driver passing the side-stepping assembler may be the person who thinks of the improvement. Ideas should be welcomed by everyone.

Obeya

Obeya meetings are similar in some respects to formal status meetings, but they are not the same. The intent is to shorten the time frame along the path of planning, working, checking or testing, responding to issues, and moving the project to success. In many respects this fits quite well with SCRUM methodology.

The concept is to present work and project status visually and track dynamically so that issues, risks and successes are noted and posted, worked, resolved, recognized. Responsible people are identified with their work so that this visibility enhances commitment, accountability, teamwork and accomplishments. If someone is accountable for work but has legitimate conflicts, others can know and see what they can do to help. Sometimes in organizations this type of opportunity to help others goes unnoticed because there is no Obeya visual identification.

Obeya sessions are intended to be just long enough to know work status, who is working what, recognize successes, etc. They should not drag on. One tendency in both Obeya and formal status meetings that I encourage you to actively manage: Focus on <u>status</u> not on <u>solving</u> problems. Rather, identify the issue, responsible people, then task someone with setting a meeting to resolve – maybe even right after the Obeya session. Encourage team members to say "You're pursuing a solution here. Let's focus on status then solve the problem later." Again, everyone should be empowered and expected to create a value-oriented work environment by doing this.

Hansei

This is a reflection of how well things have worked and suggestions for improvement. Hansei sessions can be dynamic with participants encouraged to write on white boards or post-its. It is an active discussion that should be lead by a facilitator or moderator. While Kaizan is continuous improvement, Hansei contributes to improvement by reflecting over longer sessions, processes, an entire project, etc. In this respect, themes can be gleaned from similar thoughts across multiple people and work groups. Priorities can be evaluated and opportunities for improvement planned.

Chapter 6:   Work Breakdown Structure Discovery Sessions

Creating a project management work environment should include the several steps that begin with identifying work and culminate in a project work task schedule. In my view these steps are additional facilitating processes. I present them separate from the other facilitating processes because they are tightly coupled and provide a great line-of-sight for team members to understand their importance to structuring work. This pays dividends when the same steps, although shorter and more focused, need to be used to analyze a change request during the middle of a project.

The three main activities are to develop the Work Breakdown Structure (WBS), then add detail to produce a WBS Dictionary, then use the WBS Dictionary to develop a project work task schedule. I've been amazed even in structured project environments that this straightforward sequence was not used, yet laborious schedule adjustments were accepted expectations of projects. This is another example where staff need to think of a time exchange. By spending time up front to define work reasonably well they will be saving time later in the project.

Here is a brief description followed by a more detailed example.

First, Develop the WBS: This is a listing of work from high-level to a meaningful low level. The usual guideline is between 20-40 hours of work or work tasks that require check-offs to ensure they are completed. Tasks are organized in an outline structure, i.e. from high level to secondary level to tertiary level, etc. The work is grouped by areas, e.g. electrical, design and blue print, procurement, etc.

Second, add detail to the WBS to create the WBS Dictionary. The WBS Dictionary includes a brief description of the task, why it is needed or sequenced where it is, which person or role is responsible, hours and duration as in 40 hours over three weeks, dependencies and risks.

Third, use the WBS Dictionary to create a work task schedule. Key factors from the WBS Dictionary are sequence dependencies, hours and duration and, who does the work. You can probably envision that the schedule progresses from initial work to final inspections, including the total duration and estimated completion dates for each deliverable and the entire project.

Before we look at these in detail, I can envision objections that in some environments work 6-months out can't be known in detail and can't be estimated with any accuracy. Actually, that is fine. In fact, I would tell team members that is GREAT! Here is why:

- First, they know that much.
- Second they know more needs to be learned before they can provide more accuracy.
- Third, the durations and dates are only <u>estimates</u>.
- Fourth, they can include placeholder tasks – reminders or checkpoints – to review estimates at certain points during the work.

So, rather than avoiding adding detail because not enough is known, use the situation to "work to know" so the team can then "work what they know".

Now, let's look at each phase in detail.

Work Breakdown Structure Discovery

Creating work task assignments versus managing a work task schedule is one great misconception about the role of project managers. <u>Project managers do not create work tasks</u>. Team members, who do the work, create work tasks. Project managers facilitate or lead team members through the WBS discovery exercise. Then project managers build a work task schedule based on the tasks team members identify. This is a crucial point. If tasks are created by people other than the workers, then these can be interpreted as dictates and will probably not be accurate nor sufficient.

A project management work environment with a focus on adding value requires involving the Right People at the Right Time to do the Right Work in the Right Way. This includes involving the right people to identify and create the work tasks. Only the people who know the work are qualified to be the Right People during the WBS discovery process. This could be a team lead for a unit because they would be knowledgeable and proficient with that team's work.

So, how does the WBS discovery process work?

You can use WBS software packages that come with instructions. We'll step through the process manually here so you understand the logic and so you know how to do this without software.

The process uses a common outline scheme with a high-level category, under which are secondary categories, under which are tertiary categories, etc. For example planning tasks for your company outing and meal:

I. Plan the barbeque
    a. Decide on the meats
    b. Decide on the sauces
II. Plan the dishes
    a. Appetizers
    b. Main dishes
    c. Salads
    d. Desserts
        i. Frozen
        ii. Chocolate
        iii. Fruity
III. Location setup

Step 1: Identify high-level or primary-level activities. These probably represent organizational functions like Purchasing, etc. and should include all aspects of the project. Don't divert attention by thinking about sequencing and dependencies right now. Keep attention on identifying tasks. These are some major areas in most organizations.

- Purchasing tasks
- Logistics tasks
- Legal contracts
- Promotion tasks
- Requirements gathering

Use a white-board, post-its, 3" X 5" cards or something similar to capture these major task categories. I actually prefer using physical media rather than software because the tactile nature and writing process helps create a more active, fun and team bonding experience than using software. Then use this media for adding content from the following steps.

Step 2: Identify subtasks within each primary-level. Again, focus on task identification not on sequencing or other dependencies, unless they come naturally. Here are some subtasks within Purchasing and Logistics.

I. Purchasing
    a. Identify products.
    b. Identify vendors.
    c. Identify production cycles.
    d. Determine our rollout cycles.
        i.   Initial
        ii. Annual or semi-annual
        iii. By company division
    e. Follow asset management accounting
        i.   Prepare asset management tag orders
        ii. Provide asset management tags to vendor
II. Logistics
    a. Determine delivery locations.
    b. Determine delivery providers
        i.   Internal shipping
        ii. External provider
    c. Determine insurance levels per product
        i.   Self-insured or purchase insurance
        ii. Any items not to insure?

    d. Determine delivery facilities at locations
        i. Road accesses to facilities
       ii. Restrictions from municipality or road construction
     iii. Are Alternative arrangements needed?

Step 3: Analyze the WBS tasks to determine if they are complete or should be:

- Subdivided further.

- Reorganized. For example: From the outline scheme above: should I.e.: follow "asset management accounting", be performed before I.b. "identify vendors". Perhaps lead time to complete asset management accounting means this should be completed before identifying vendors.

- Clarified with any notes or even reworded completely.

Step 4: Organize the tasks into their logical sequence based upon which tasks should be completed first through last. Let's say the only change is to shift I.e. up to become I.b.

I. Purchasing
    a. Identify products.
    b. Follow asset management accounting
        i. Prepare asset management tag orders
       ii. Provide asset management tags to vendor
    c. Identify vendors.
    d. Identify production cycles.
    e. Determine our rollout cycles.
       iii. Initial
       iv. Annual or semi-annual
       v. By company division

Step 5: Organize and sequence tasks across primary-task categories. To do this analyze dependencies between Purchasing tasks and Logistics tasks. Make notes on the media or other source that can be "parking lot" action items to complete following the working sessions.

These dependencies will be included in the project work task schedule so that if something affects one task, all dependent tasks can be shifted also.

Step 6: Label the media, whether white board, post-its, 3" X 5" cards, etc. with the outline numbering scheme so that the sequence can be transferred to a scheduling tool.

That is it. Of course, the work task schedule may be refined as the project progresses. This is natural, but these changes should be refinements not wholesale changes.

You may be wondering why I consider this a facilitating process. The answer is that in the absence of such a structured process each of the key pieces would happen ad-hoc over weeks or months rather than in a couple of hours. Consider what this activity accomplishes:

- Identifying tasks
- Identifying dependencies
- Building team affiliation and commitment
- Organizing tasks in a meaningful sequence
- Framing all of the work parts so that each team member can understand the whole project, the component pieces and how they fit.
- All this reinforces that the project team is working together to add value to your organization.

In the absence of such a structured process, team members can become frustrated with chaos, frustrated with each other, frustrated with rework, i.e. your organization builds contention rather than commitment. An abbreviated example of how this example would look using white board, post-its or other media is presented below. Notice that the highest level tasks are at the top. Sequence follows top down within a work category and left to right across work categories.

Figure 13: Work Breakdown Structure Initial Organization

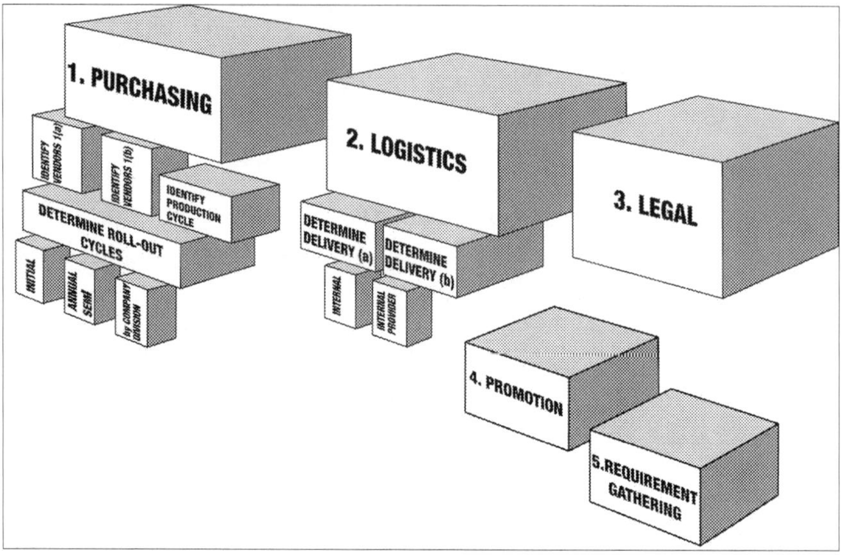

WBS Dictionary development

This is a straightforward and logical extension of the WBS. As I mentioned earlier, additional detail is added. Here is a sample WBS Dictionary structure, that is fairly intuitive, with enough information to help get you started. A blank template is also included in the Appendix.

Table 4: WBS Dictionary Sample

Task & Hierarchy	Hours / Duration	Role or Person	Details	Dependencies	Risks	Risk Mitigation
Purchasing I	(Summary Task: Sum of all sub tasks.)	Marcia	Purchasing has established relationships.	Requirements. Vendor product availability	No products meet all requirements.	Prioritize requirements as musts and optional.
Identify Products I.a	5 hours over 2 days.	Marcia	Evaluate products against specifications.	Sufficient requirements. Sufficient vendor information.	Selecting an inadequate product if vendor information does not address all requirements.	Require presentation and Q/A session with vendor engineers, not just sales.
Identify Vendors I.b	5 hours over 2 days at same time as	Norm	Post request for information for potential vendors.	Vendor products exist. Vendors interested in volume and conditions.	No vendor has a product that meets <u>must-have</u> requirements.	Notify sponsors to determine project viability and options.
Identify Production Cycles I.c	10 hours over 2 weeks.	Norm	Production cycles can affect availability and provide end of life buy specials.	Depends on how fast vendors return requests. Can't begin until Vendors are identified.	Preferred Vendor does not respond timely.	Select from alternate vendors.
Determine rollout cycles I.d	(Summary Task. Sum of all sub-tasks.)	Norm	What are factors that impact our rollout to end users?	Clients need to provide their needs.	Clients do not decide in time to meet vendor production window.	Involve client in all phases of selection and require client approval for rollout schedules.
Initial I.d.i	5 hours over 2 days.	Norm	What is our initial rollout and does this match vendor production cycle and volume?	Vendor typically need a 2-week minimum lead time. 3-months for volume greater than 5,000 units.	Clients do not decide in time to meet vendor production window	Replan schedule based on when clients decide.
Annual or semi I.d.ii	5 hours over 2 days – concurrent with I.d.i	Norm	Should our rollout be continuous or otherwise?	Clients need to provide their needs.	Clients do not decide in time to meet vendor production window	Replan schedule based on when clients decide.
By company or division I.d.iii	5 hours over 2 days – concurrent with I.d.i	Norm	Should rollouts be by division or company-wide?	Clients need to provide their needs.	Clients do not decide in time to meet vendor production window	Replan schedule based on when clients decide.

Schedule development

Scheduling flows logically from the WBS Dictionary information. Use whichever tool is in your organization, such as MS-Project, Primavera, etc.. Simply transpose the tasks, durations, sequencing and dependencies to the scheduling tool. If your organization does not have a scheduling tool, the schedule can be developed in a spreadsheet format. Because the focus of this book is adding value using project management principles, I'm not addressing scheduling tools, capabilities, tracking, baselining, etc. Again, plenty of other books cover this in detail. With that in mind, here are a few more principles about schedules.

Consider the schedule as a formal document that is authorized. The schedule can adjust to flex with reality. Remember it is a tool so, use the schedule (play the ball) – don't let the schedule control you (don't let the ball play you). However, authorizing the schedule allows you to control conscious and intentional work delays. I've experienced organizations changing their priorities, saying: "We need to delay the project for a month." If this is allowed, your company could be paying for a project team during the month of downtime with no way to be compensated. This would be a major impact that should be managed with formal change control. Authorizing the schedule provides one additional weapon in your arsenal to protect the project from adverse impact. An intentional change to the schedule should be evaluated, impacts understood and approved.

One other point about schedules. Remember that the entire purpose and focus of project management principles are to help complete work that adds value. The work schedule is simply another tool for this purpose. I advise that you use it this way. I have seen effective schedules written on sheets of paper and tracked manually. I've also seen complicated schedules that are micromanaged to the point where particular details of each task become the focus, rather than tasks contributing to adding value.

Chapter 7:   Metrics

Overview

In some respects this chapter is longer than I intended for this type of book. On the other hand, metrics are soooo important that I wanted to err on the side of more information than less. Hang in with me as you read the chapter. Because metrics involve multiple components and some calculations, take your time to work through this section. Try using your own data and get a feel for the metrics. I think you'll understand the value.

Metrics are an extremely important feature in an organization. Probably second only to the organization's core business itself. Metrics exist at a financial level to demonstrate revenue, expenses and profits. They exist at asset levels for inventory, product flow, order triggers and shelf life. Metrics also exist at the level organizations need to measure aspects like:

- How effectively staff work to complete deliverables, whether a print run or installing an assembly system.

- Whether expenses remain high following a project because defects are found for several months.

- Reinforcing the value of processes to guide work.

- Costs that continue after a project is supposedly over – although most organizations don't have ways of measuring this. The best way is to include a "in operation" phase that lasts for a couple months.

You can probably think of many metrics you wish your organization generated that could add value. An entire set of metrics exists within project management. Here are some samples:

- <u>Schedule progress</u>, i.e. will the project finish on time or how far ahead of schedule is it?

- <u>Cost comparison</u> to an overall budget, per contracts, per deliverables, etc.

- <u>Quality measurements</u> that indicate if what is being build is meeting specifications.

- <u>Hours</u> spent to produce each deliverable.

Think of these project metrics as analogous to operational and finance metrics. Your organization should take time to determine which project metrics you want to capture. Then you can plan how to capture them, who will be assigned which metrics, reporting frameworks, etc. Honestly, implementing metrics is one of the most valuable accomplishments for your organization. Benefits will include that your organization can be managed by metrics, by facts, rather than by hunches and anecdotes. Also, project managers actually relish the opportunity to plan projects to the extent that metrics can be calculated, reported and used to manage work. Partner with your project managers to do this and watch your return on investment climb.

More about identifying, capturing and using metrics later. Now, I want to present standard project management metrics, then some ideas for custom metrics. These standard project management metrics require several contributing factors.

<u>First, sufficient planning</u> so that work is defined and estimated by the people who will be doing it, can be managed effectively and, so that tasks are scheduled at a meaningful level. If project tasks are too high level or by someone other than those who know the work, then a set of 8 tasks that are scheduled for one week can easily grow to 18 tasks that take a month and involve five additional people. Trained project managers can facilitate effective planning, so involve them as early as possible.

<u>Second, a commitment to record keeping</u> so that data is current and accurate throughout the project. This is a simple "gold in, gold out" versus "garbage in, garbage out" principle. Metric accuracy and meaningfulness is dependent on the accuracy of the data used to calculate the metrics. Options exist for producing fairly accurate data even if your organization does not have automated or precise

methods to record time. For example a spreadsheet can be used to list work tasks to the nearest 15 minutes. This is an arbitrary interval so, you can make this 5 minutes or a tenth of an hour if you want. Making record keeping straightforward, easy and meaningful for employees is the best way to develop the commitment to it. The more difficult or confusing the less likely employees will use it and the less accurate the data. Also, don't worry too much about rounding to the nearest N minutes. Based on the law of averages and the principle of a generalized distribution around an average, this rounding should work pretty well.

<u>Third, a reasonable amount of time and effort</u> to produce the metrics. You may be able to automate producing some metrics while others will need to be calculated either by hand or via formulas entered in a spreadsheet. Presenting data from the previous week during current week status meetings is not unusual so, don't feel the pressure to have up-to-the-day metrics or you'll end up running yourself and others ragged to meet an arbitrary weekly deadline.

Again, set expectations within your organization for these contributing factors. As your organization matures its work environment, these contributing factors will become more ingrained and part of managing work.

Standard project management metrics

This section can't just be read in a continual flow. You'll need to think about it, digest it, work through some formulas. The value is that you'll understand how metrics will let you add value by measuring progress and managing using these metrics.

Let's use a simple example of fencing a lot. Installing the fence around all four sides is estimated to cost $12,000 and take 12 days or 3 days per side. This equates to a budgeted value of $1,000 per day and $3,000 per side. If each post and section of fence represented $100 then each side would have 30 posts. Here is a visual:

Figure 14: Building a Fence Cost Metrics Example

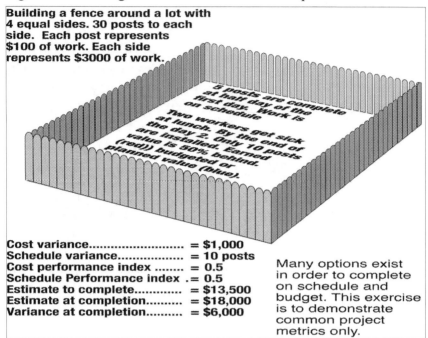

Building a fence around a lot with 4 equal sides. 30 posts to each side. Each post represents $100 of work. Each side represents $3000 of work.

5 posts are complete at half day of the first day. Work is on schedule.

Two workers get sick at lunch. By the end of the day 2. Only 10 posts are installed. Earned value is 50% behind. planned value (blue).

Cost variance............................ = $1,000
Schedule variance.................... = 10 posts
Cost performance index .... = 0.5
Schedule Performance index .= 0.5
Estimate to complete............. = $13,500
Estimate at completion.......... = $18,000
Variance at completion.......... = $6,000

Many options exist in order to complete on schedule and budget. This exercise is to demonstrate common project metrics only.

Budget at Completion: The budget to complete the work or $12,000.

Earned Value: This is the amount of value that has been 'earned' to a certain point based upon the estimated budget. This statistic involves both cost and schedule. A daily rate of 10 posts would equal 100% of earned value. Say that at half-day or lunch of the first day 5 posts were installed and represents $500 of value. The project is on schedule.

However, two workers get sick from lunch and miss the rest of the day and the second day so that only 10 posts are installed at end of day 2. Earned value = 10 X $100 = $1,000, instead of the $2,000 value expected by end of the second day.

Cost Variance

Cost variance is the difference between budgeted value and earned value. Earned value at day 2 equals $1,000 - $2,000 = -$1,000. The project has spent $1,000 more to this point than budgeted. Cost variance can be calculated at various points through the project. If project work can be spread across all work fairly evenly – sometimes a big assumption – then both earned value and cost variance can be determined at a discrete level, e.g. per day.

Note: Astute readers like you are probably saying: "Whoa, not so fast." The cost variance has to account for not paying the two workers who are out sick." Well, not necessarily if sick day compensation is included. For the sake of this example, let's keep the accounting simple and say that sick day compensation is included so, the budgeted costs are the same.

Schedule Variance

Schedule variance is the difference between the expected or budgeted and actual duration; often in terms of hours, days or weeks. In this case the budgeted schedule would be completing 20 posts at the end of day two. The variance is calculated as actual (10) minus budgeted (10) = -10. The project work is behind by 10 posts.

Cost Performance Index

Cost performance index is the percent of budgeted cost to a certain point compared with the actual or earned cost. The formula is actual / earned. In this case the cost performance index = $1,000 / $2,000 = 0.5 or 50%. A perfect index would be 1.0 or 100%. Extending this out to day three, the budgeted or expected budget is $3,000 which can be multiplied by 0.5 = $1,500 at the end of day three.

Schedule Performance Index

Schedule performance index is the percent of the scheduled work that has been completed. In this case 10 posts are completed compared to 20 posts so, the schedule performance index = 10 / 20 = 0.5 or 50%. A perfect index would be 1.0 or 100%.

Why are cost performance index and schedule performance index important? Because these metrics can help indicate the status of the work in order to manage the remainder of the work by doing things like, extending the completion date, adding more workers to catch up, getting more power equipment to dig holes and install posts faster or asking for more money. Managing by metrics is a big deal, but can't be done if the metrics are not calculated.

Estimate to Complete

Estimate to complete is calculated by extrapolating the earned value for the remainder of the project by using the cost and schedule performance indexes. If the two sick workers do not return or are not replaced, the rate of work would reasonably continue to be half of the budgeted work every two days. The project is scheduled to cost the original $3,000 by end of day three, plus $1,500 additional dollars for a total of $4,500 for side one.

The remaining three sides would also cost an additional $1,500. Calculated:

Budgeted cost for sides 2, 3, 4 = $3,000 X 3 = $9,000.

Estimated cost increase for each side = $1,500 X 3 = $4,500

Estimate to complete the remainder of the work = $9,000 + $4,500 = $13,500

Estimate at Completion

The estimate at completion is the total of the estimate to complete plus the costs to that point, also called sunk costs. In this example: $13,500 + $4,500 = $18,000.

Variance at Completion

The variance at completion is the budget at completion minus the estimate at completion. In this example $12,000 - $18,000 = -$6,000.

Cumulative Cost Performance Index

Cumulative cost performance index is the cumulate percent at successive stages of work. This could indicate trends that are arithmetic or geometric. Often graphs are terrific tools to present these types of relationships. For our simple example, the cumulative cost performance index is equal to the standard cost performance index.

Return on Investment

Return on investment is based on the value of the completed work over some duration. Let's say the fenced lot is to store securely recreational vehicles like boats or motor homes or, to provide a large dog park for exercise. The return on investment would equal the sunk costs of the deliverable or project at completion divided by the income. Recovering the sunk costs may take 12 months with a steady profit after month 12.

Internal Rate of Return

Internal rate of return is the financial return compared to other internal costs, i.e. loans used to construct the fence. If the revenue from renting the lot = $1,000 per month and your organization is paying $800 per month for the loan then the internal rate of return is $200 per month.

Metric meaningfulness

The meaningfulness of these metrics really depends on each project. As much as I promote metrics, I also say that they are tools to help people manage things; in this case manage work. So, taking an adage from ball sports – play the ball, don't' let the ball play you. You are in control. Use the metrics but don't let the metrics lead you into forcing their use where not really appropriate.

All metrics are great for managing large and complex projects. However, some are not really worth the overhead for small and uncomplicated projects. Examples:

- A project to conduct an employee opinion survey during two months within a small organization, say less than 200 people, could benefit from some straightforward metrics like cost variance and schedule variance. However the project would probably be near completion before metrics like cost performance index and schedule performance index would help manage the work. That said, all metrics could be used after a project completes to evaluate how well the work was planned and executed. Evaluation like this can be used to plan and execute the next project more effectively.

- A project to design and install a fire-suppression system into an existing five-story building could benefit from all of these metrics.

  o It would take long enough that all scheduling metrics would provide value.
  o It would involve purchasing enough materials to justify using budget and cost metrics.
  o It has sufficient improvement value to calculate return on investment and internal rate of return metrics.

So, the point is that one size does not fit all. Use the metrics that fit the nature of the project, but DO USE METRICS. Hold project managers and sponsors accountable for defining, gathering the data and, calculating the metrics that will be used during the project. Again, everyone in the organization should understand the value of metrics and do their part to provide the data needed to generate the metrics. This may be by recording work hours as accurately as possible each week or by saying "those facilitating processes really helped the last project move faster. Let's use them again to see if we can stay ahead of the planned schedule." Also, if managers in your organization reviewed metrics with employees the value of the metrics would be reinforced, as well as the expectation that employees do their part to help generate the metrics.

Another huge value of using metrics is reinforcement of the three key factors listed earlier:

- Sufficient planning
- Commitment to record keeping
- A reasonable amount of time and effort

Your organization will see that these really are key factors and begin building them into their daily work, project planning and estimating. People will also breath a sigh of relief knowing these actually help add value to their organization.

Additional business and operational metrics can be incorporated into a project management work environment. For example, Return on Investment (ROI), Internal Rate of Return (IRR), sunk costs, etc. These are valuable for evaluating projects within a total investment of the organization or Portfolio Management.

Custom metrics

Two colleagues from different organizations are in a cross-company mentoring program, and are comparing features of how work is accomplished.

Dean: "We were able to start 10 separate work efforts last year (let's call these projects) that we estimate represent 40,000 hours of work."

Teresa: "Wow, you started 10! How long did the initiation time take? We've found a strong relationship between prep time and completing within 10% of the estimated duration." We decided that because completion represented gaining value from money we already spent, i.e. our sunk costs, that we benefit more from starting only the work that is planned sufficiently and that we know we have the staff capacity to complete.

Dean: "Don't know the initiation time. We pull in several executives and unit managers for a couple of hour discussions, then they use some templates we developed to describe and estimate the work by the next week. I'm impressed by you guys completing work within 10% of estimates. How many projects do you start each year?"

Teresa: "We increased each of the past three years. First year was low, three projects, because we learned what planning well meant the previous two years. We only start as many projects as the teams can plan adequately. This has improved each year. Second year we initiated 5 projects and still had capacity for more. This year we started 6 projects and that is about our capacity. We found that employees in the trenches actually provided the best planning information, rather than executives and unit managers alone."

Now you are pretty smart, so you can see where this scenario is headed. Custom metrics can help your organization evaluate some critical success factors of completing work to add value. Just as in this scenario, your organization can compare up-front planning with end results. This type of metric can help guide your operations by showing the value of planning. However, not capturing this type of information results in relying on anecdotes and hunches. Here are a few custom metrics, factors required to calculate them, with a quick example and conclusions for each.

Table 5: Custom Metrics Samples

Metric	Required Factors

Staff capacity. The total number of hours your staff can devote to project work. Consider these factors for calculating this metric.
• 50 weeks X 40 hours per week = 2,000 hours per employee annually.
• Subtract the number of hours for:
   o Vacation, sick and personal days.
   o Personnel development and training.
   o Maintenance work
• Subtract hours for preparation time, unless already built into your organization.
	• Staff hours-worked tracking.
	
	• Known time per staff member for vacations, sick and personal days, personnel development, maintenance work, etc.
	
	• Transition time for staff to move from one job or type of work to another. They may need to learn skills, travel, complete preparation work for equipment, safety, etc. that provides the environment to work but is not devoted to specific work tasks.

Example: Fred's team of 5 has base capacity of: 5 X 50 X 40 = 10,000 hours per year. Subtract vacation time of 14 X 40 hours; 10,000 - 460 hours = 9, 540 hours. Subtract other 10 days (sick, and personal days) per person for 50 days X 8 hours = 400 hours; 9,540 – 400 = 9,140 Subtract 600 hours per person for ongoing maintenance; 600 X 5 = 3,000 hours; 9,140 – 3,000 = 6,140. Total dedicated project work time = 6,140 hours.	• How many hours are estimated for a project? • Average hours of sick time over the past N years. • How many hours for personnel development are planned? • How many hours in unit, group, company meetings are scheduled? • Average maintenance work time during the past N years. • Preparation time, etc.
Conclusion: Approximately 60% of Fred's team's total capacity is available for dedicated project work. Scheduling more work than this will create contentions that could compromise work completion, work quality, employee related factors such as stress and company dedication. The actual amount of time available for dedicated project work is sometimes a surprise to many who have not calculated it.	

Metric	Required Factors
Recycle time for (requirements, deliverables, etc.) Using requirements as an example: How much time is used to clarify requirements, add or remove requirements, etc.	• Project work hour tracking. • Time to process, calculate and prepare reports. • Process to recognize when requirement recycle work is occurring. • Empowered employees who are encouraged and rewarded for recognizing, identifying and maybe escalating when this occurs.
Example: A client or internal business partner submits a work order, RFP, or equivalent, complete with deliverables and requirements. The client has budgeted 2,000 total hours at the blended work rate of $50 per hour for an estimated cost of $100,000. The client does not want to spend time reviewing and clarifying requirements because they already spent 250 hours developing the work order. The work is accepted. After one month a solution approach is presented to the client who says the requirements have been misinterpreted and wants to meet with the team to clarify. This happens iteratively throughout the project, resulting in a total of 200 hours to rework requirements. Rework time = 200 X $50 = $10,000 or 10% of the project estimated cost.	• Team members remind the client this was recommended before work began. • The project team needs to track both preparation time and actual time spent in meetings, telephone calls, travel, etc. to clarify requirements. • Use a spreadsheet to track rework per requirement and deliverable. Save this in a central location for the project so it can't get deleted by mistake from someone's computer.
Conclusion: Tracking discrete metrics like this can be used to show clients the value of pausing the project before 10% of the budget is consumed in recycling work they thought was complete. If the project completes and is within a 10% reserve or contingency amount – GREAT! However, other costs can consume the reserve budget. Also, a discrete metric like this can be used to pinpoint what is causing project slippage which results in reduced earned value presented by the Standard Project Management Metrics presented earlier.	

I recommend using a two stage approach to determining custom metrics:

1. Rate the metrics as those essential or highest priority to lowest priority.

2. Incorporate them into small projects first so you gain experience, then you can institutionalize them within your organization.

Section 3: Mobility and Traction

Now that we have covered the foundation or skeleton in Section 1; the form and function in Section 2, this section focuses on mobility and traction or how the organism of your project management work environment can actually move about and gain a critical mass of experience to add value and become self-reinforcing. OK, the organism analogy may be a stretch, but I think you can see the importance of building a foundation, applying a structure for functionality, then letting it move and gain traction in your organization.

Chapter 8:   Methodologies

I struggle with methodologies because, while they do provide steps and sequences, they can seem restrictive rather than freeing and enabling. Using a methodology maturely can require several years experience. Team members wonder which phase the project is in, which rules apply, can the methodology adapt for projects that are unique compared to the 'normal' projects. Again, I really like the analogy from ball sports to "Play the ball, don't let the ball play you." A methodology is a tool to use, not to be bound by and restricted.

So, a legitimate question is: What value do methodologies provide? In fact, considering that you are pretty clever I can understand you restating the two foundational questions from Chapter 1 for methodologies:

- What do you <u>want</u> methodologies to do for your project management work environment?
- What are your <u>assumptions</u> about methodologies?

Great questions.

What methodologies provide

Methodologies should provide measures of control appropriate for your industry and types of work. Consequently, I <u>want</u> methodologies to provide <u>mobility</u>; to get the work moving and keep it moving. Road construction projects will have a different methodology than software development projects. Nuclear engineering projects will have a different methodology than marketing projects. So while all work flows through the five phases described earlier, methodologies need to provide a lot of other functional details appropriate for each type of work.

However, this does not mean that methodologies must be complicated. In fact, you'll see shortly that methodologies can be fairly simple and easy to use. But first, what are some assumptions – to answer the second question.

My assumptions about methodologies are that:

- <u>Methodologies make sense and are intuitive</u> to people in your organization.

   Your staff should not be confused by your methodology. Rather they should see it as a natural fit. This will also avoid the potential for 'paralysis by analysis'.

- <u>Methodologies can incorporate the foundational form and function components</u> seamlessly.

   Your staff should not need to learn complicated intricacies but should be able to say "I see the big picture and how component parts fit so that we add value in the best way possible."

- <u>Methodologies are flexible</u> rather than rigid.

   If a project does not quite fit the usual type of work, staff should be able to see how to adjust without major agony and mental contortions.

Four main methodology factors

I have led work using a variety of methodologies; complex, rigid, flexible and too loose. My conclusion is that methodologies amount to letting the work progress, i.e. mobility based on these factors:

- Is the work defined adequately and understood by everyone the same way?

  This includes scope statements, deliverable descriptions and requirements. Inevitably someone will say something like: "Well, we always understood and expected that we'd get to the point in the project where we could add these features or do these things." This indicates that portion of the work is not defined adequately so, the work for that portion should pause until this is resolved. The slogan "work to know, then work what you know" applies here. Hey, facilitating processes can help with this!

- Are dependencies and risks known and being managed?

  Every dependency that is not managed presents a risk that subsequent work can't begin. Other specific risks, like whether impacts during a 12-month outdoor construction project, need to be identified and mitigation steps planned. Specific management plans are the best way to ensure dependencies are known and risks are being managed.

- Are discrete steps or phases known and provide quality check points?

  The divisions between software application design, development, testing and deployment steps are a good example. Looking at these in dependency order:
    o Deployment should not begin until all testing is complete and approved to the standards of those who deploy.
    o Testing should not begin until all development is complete and approved to the expectations of

those who perform testing.
  o Development should not begin until designs are approved by those who need to write software code.
  o Design should not begin until deliverables and requirements are defined well enough to be accepted by those who design.
  o This pattern can be extended to any industry.
- <u>Can the methodology accommodate the management plan?</u>

  For example, the change request process should incorporate easily into the methodology. Also, the management plan includes roles and responsibilities, covered in the next chapter, so these should be inherent to the methodology.

These are what I consider the four main factors for any methodology. So, because I really struggle with methodologies, what do I recommend? <u>I recommend letting the project core team determine the methodology</u>. They know the nature of the work, the subject matter and specific industry. They can recognize the steps, cycles, and controls that are needed to get the work moving, keep it moving with quality, and complete it to provide value for your organization.

What about if your organization does not have experience with a methodology? How can they determine a methodology to use without a frame of reference? Ohh, I like that question! My recommendation for this frame of reference is either SCRUM or Rolling Wave. Also, I really like the Technical Readiness Levels developed by NASA. These are presented below.

Also, I can hear skeptics say that if team members control the methodology, they'll take shortcuts, succumb to pressure from executives to make compromises and meet arbitrary deadlines or commitments promised by sales or others who aren't doing the work. Note that I did not say to let only the <u>work team</u> decide but to let the <u>core team</u> decide. The core team includes the sponsor, project manager, team leads, foremen, supervisors, etc. All members of the core team should have a voice to present their reasons because most people have good reasons that affect how well they can do their jobs.

Oh, also remember that the project manager and team should have autonomy to run the project based on the methodology.

Fortunately, a methodology already exists that both fits this model, provides a framework and will help your organization gain experience so that future work can be mobilized and guided appropriately. In my opinion SCRUM is this methodology. I do not present it as a panacea, but read below to see if it might work for you.

SCRUM Methodology

The methodology that I think meets all four factors and provides the best combination of mobility and control is SCRUM. Scrum is a specific Agile methodology that focuses on short, deliverable phases called sprints. Think of a rugby scrum with team members shoulder to shoulder working together. Key features are:

- Determining the deliverables.
- Deciding on the length of a deliverable phase (Sprint). Thirty days, 60 days, 90 days, etc.
- Deciding on sequencing deliverables, i.e. which comes first, second, third, etc. Those in the current sprint are worked. Others are said to be in a "backlog", as would be any approved new deliverables.
- Small teams that work together to plan, build, test, deliver.
- Low overhead because the work is divided into short deliverables.
- Effective management, communication, metrics and reporting are all inherent with SCRUM.

Many sources are available to learn SCRUM, complete with rules, steps, tracking, team roles and authority, etc. I really like SCRUM for three main reasons:

- It <u>focuses on discrete deliverables</u> so, success is evident, measurable and self-reinforcing.

- Focusing on discrete deliverables within an agreed time frame, called a "sprint", causes everyone to <u>think in project management terms</u> of defining the work, planning the work, protecting the work from risks and changes and, delivering the work within the time frame.

- These discrete deliverables can actually be documents like the project Charter, Plan, Metrics, etc. in addition to major deliverables such as a solenoid control unit.

- <u>Changes to an existing deliverable can be incorporated during subsequent Sprints</u>. This is a great inherent change control mechanism. Think of the conversation: "Can we add this to the project?" Answer: "Next sprint starts in two weeks. Propose it so the team can determine the priority and what is needed to complete it. If approved, it will be sequenced and delivered in the appropriate sprint phase."

Other benefits include:

- SCRUM can actually fit annual work cycles often called 'releases'. Let's say your organization implements new features, products, prototypes, etc. on a monthly or bi-monthly cycle. Scrum methodology is ideal for adding the rigor and structure needed to manage work within these cycles, reducing implementation slippage.

- SCRUM complements work capacity management. Staff can cycle through a deliverable then move on to other work as needed. Each phase is short enough that planning the next phase is manageable against factors like the available staff and other work priorities.

Rolling Wave

Rolling wave is quite similar to SCRUM in several respects, although SCRUM purists may not agree with this. Rolling wave operates by planning work in phases, then replanning the remaining work at regular intervals or points. The remaining work should be replanned when the current phase completes. In my estimation, the only real difference between Rolling Wave and SCRUM is the formality of SCRUM in its pure form. However, both use the concept of breaking work into phases based on completing deliverables then planning to complete the next set of deliverables.

In fairness to other methodologies and options, two common methodologies are presented below.

Waterfall methodology

Think of work progressing through a series of waterfalls. Work tasks are grouped as high-level categories that progress sequentially. Work in a downstream category does not begin until all the tasks are complete in an upstream category. Consider a bridge maintenance project. Sequential categories could be:

1. Planning
    a. Evaluate structural integrity.
    b. Identify maintenance activities.
    c. Monitor traffic activity.
2. Prepare for bridge work
    a. Order parts and equipment.
    b. Determine traffic control operations.
    c. Prepare bridge sections for maintenance.
3. Development
    a. Structural integrity maintenance work.
    b. Surface preparation and painting.
4. Clean up
    a. Remove equipment.
    b. Remove traffic control

Figure 15: Waterfall Workflow Example

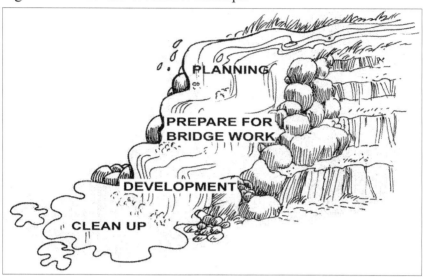

<u>Category 1 Planning</u> tasks would need to complete prior to beginning <u>Category 2 Prepare for bridge work</u> tasks and the same for <u>Development</u> and <u>Clean-up</u> tasks.

While this provides sequential controls, the level of control in a waterfall methodology is not always practical. For example, your project team may need to place orders for some parts and equipment months ahead of completing all <u>Planning</u> tasks. Otherwise, the time needed to receive the parts and equipment could really delay work. Similarly, a traffic control plan could be developed based on recent historical information from a county or city without needing to wait for all <u>Planning</u> tasks to complete.

Waterfall is quite practical for many smaller, limited scope projects because it is logical and not much time is wasted. However, Waterfall methodology can also flex based on dependencies. I've managed projects in which separate parts of the work needed to be Waterfall while other parts could operate independently. They just needed to be coordinated intelligently, e.g. by knowing dependencies, so they came together at the right time. This gets closer to Agile Methodology which is designed for flexibility, particularly for projects with moderate to high complexity. As a colleague said: "I just returned from Agile training. I'm glad to know that I've been doing it for decades by modifying a Waterfall schedule as needed to accommodate the work."

Agile methodology

An Agile methodology provides flexibility to perform work tasks based upon dependencies for each task. Also, the elephant of a larger project is eaten one segment or deliverable at a time within short duration iterations. Each work segment or deliverable is defined, planned, built, tested, delivered, then the team moves to the next work segment. Using the bridge maintenance project example again, task 3 in Planning: monitoring traffic activity is not dependent on evaluating structural integrity so, it can actually begin at the same time or earlier. Similarly, from the outset your team knows sandblasting equipment is needed to prepare metal for painting. Because sand is readily available, an adequate amount of sand can be ordered immediately with more sand delivered as needed.

Agile is a type of methodology developed and used primarily for software development, but many organizations have modified it to fit the nature of their work. Many great resources on the internet describe Agile in detail. Purists may wince at my description, but information from purists are readily available for when you need that level of detail.

Pick a methodology, but USE IT

Many other methodologies exist and are specific to industries or more appropriate for manufacturing or research and development operations. Some companies use multiple methodologies. Also, other systems exist to manage work and provide quality controls. Six Sigma and Lean are two others.

I really like what one colleague advocated: That no matter what methodology is selected, use a methodology. I agree. Don't make selecting a methodology too big a deal. Find one and use it. Gain experience and tweak it. Make it work for you.

So, from these fairly popular methodologies you can see that any methodology can work. The best methodology for your organization is up to you. One company I worked for used a custom methodology developed by a consulting company. Even though it was well documented and training was provided, it contained so many options, so many steps and so much repetition that many workers felt it created paralysis by analysis. I told project manager colleagues in this environment that in the hands of an experienced project manager, the methodology can do whatever is needed. I still believe that because I operate by the principle to "play the ball, don't let the ball play you."

I encourage you to find an existing, industry accepted methodology and add as few unique features as possible. Why use an industry accepted methodology? First, training your staff and developing their maturity will be easier because training and tools will exist. Paying for this type of training is far less costly than developing your own methodology or using one that is not industry accepted. Second, your organization will be able to work much easier with other organizations, such as vendors, clients and consultants, because they will also be familiar with industry standard methodologies. In fact, if your organization often uses consultants or vendors, you could adopt their methodology. If they don't have a set methodology, have them adopt yours.

Progressing work within your own organization:

Starting points and controlled progression within units or teams

Most work within an organization can be divided into building something new versus managing or changing something that already exists. Both present their own challenges. Creating something new often means working backward from a vision of a finished product until all the component pieces are decomposed and a logical development sequence can be scheduled. Adding functionality to an existing product or service is disruptive to some degree. So, the emphasis is on adding the new functionality without compromising the integrity of what exists. This holds true whether adding a window to a house, a traffic control light to an intersection or a new muffler system to an engine. An entire book can be dedicated to this topic, but I'm not headed down that path right now.

Effective planning and developing a set of procedures or steps that ensure quality, can decrease the disruption and, that is the essential part of this section – instituting systematic processes that guide the progression of work to maximize quality while minimizing disruption.

If your organization has not formally developed starting points and stages of progression within your units, you'll really benefit from this. In fact, my experience is that team members have loads of experience with what works and what to avoid that they are eager to establish progressions. These progressions provide stability and consistency. They also feed into project planning and work activity scheduling because the team's know:

- The reasonable time frame required for each step and total sequence
- Interaction points or dependencies of their work with other work.

As mentioned in Chapter 6, Facilitating Process, modeling is a great tool for determining work progressions and sequences.

The concept of entry criteria

Project work will probably need to flow across teams within your organization. For example from initial sketches to graphic design to development or prototyping to testing, printing or manufacturing, etc. A common problem is each team may not know what the next team needs to do their work. How detailed does a design need to be in order for prototyping to build a working model? Does a team need 3-D diagrams? Are temperature tolerances needed to select materials? Are energy input and output needed and should these be in electrical units or thermal units?

Oh yes teams will know some details, but will they know necessary and sufficient details? Remember that the devil is in the details and just a few missed key details can make a huge difference. Now you may be thinking, "We've already read that if project management processes are followed, then these details should be discovered in planning, so why the discussion here?" I like the question. It shows you are thinking in the right direction.

If the project has been managed correctly then all this will be known and what is produced in each unit will match what the next unit needs. The goal is for each unit to develop "entry criteria" or what they need to do their work. These criteria should then be provided downstream to all units that would want to send work their way.

While managing software development and IT projects I developed a concept in which the subsequent area defined what it needed from the previous area. If those criteria were not met then the product could not advance. Implementing this type of control requires agreement by a lot of people in an organization and may require several intermediate controls and reviews. For example, a testing unit needs to know the tests, the test protocols, parameters, product specifications, etc. These are the criteria to enter testing. The unit providing the product for testing is responsible for providing all of these specifications. If the entry criteria are not known then they can't be provided.

If work flows from right to left.

Then control flows in the opposite direction.

Figure 16: Control Flows Reverse of Work Flow

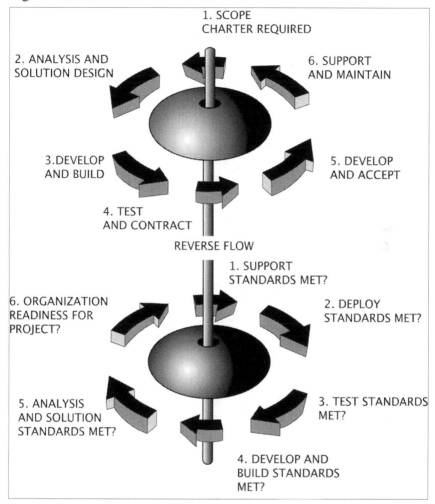

If all of the teams communicated with each other well and if your organization has meaningful interrelationships among the teams then this type of planning would happen fairly seamlessly. Reality is that each of these teams are probably within different organizational units and they receive work requests and provide services to many other units within your organization. So, this is not always easy.

Project management analysis and planning looks for these type of dependencies, but the best way is to build them into your company so that projects can automatically include them, the time frames, costs, etc. Instituting these in your company also allows measuring repeated steps and process to determine averages, standard deviations, etc. so each set of work becomes more predictable.

Examples of work progression

Fortunately these concepts have been developed within several fields. Your organization may be using them, which would be great. I want to share two examples for you here:

- Software development life cycle
- Technical Readiness Levels developed by NASA and the DoD

Software Development Life Cycle

Again, a lot of sources are on the internet and I encourage you to look at them for ideas. Some methodologies include software development lifecycles and you already know that Agile and SCRUM were developed for software development. The real value regardless of your industry, is to gain an understanding of how to develop a logical and controlled progression of work for your organization. Remember to think of end-to-end costs not just when the software is delivered. Also, software development is a great environment to apply the "Value of Finding Defects Early vs. Late" tool in chapter 10.

Technical Readiness Levels (TRL) from NASA and DoD

Many engineering and manufacturing organizations have adopted this and customized it to fit their needs. Here are two sources, but just conduct an internet search and you'll find many more.

http://esto.nasa.gov/files/TRL_definitions.pdf

www.**smdc.army.mil**/.../BAA/DoD-TechnologyReadinessLevels. doc

Technical readiness levels are organized from the lowest levels to highest levels. Descriptions are in Appendix G for your reference and use. The principle is to involve each customer or user with the research or development part of your organization. Develop consensus and demonstrate capabilities and validation at each step along the way. This includes multiple testing iterations.

Note that this is not easy. It requires much planning, communication, testing, questioning and ultimately costing and manufacturing data. The value is ensuring that the work progresses as it is proven out and that the customers at each stage are involved in the decision and approval process.

Your organization may not be engineering or manufacturing focused. But you can use the logical progression then extend the principles to the progression of work across units in your organization. Again, play the ball, don't let the ball play you. If only 4 levels are needed, don't develop 9 levels just because NASA did.

Recommendation: Develop this type of structure by running it as a project. Develop a charter, plan, determine sponsors, stakeholders, the entire core team. Determine deliverables and how these will be communicated. Determine an entire implementation strategy and schedule, including how employees will be trained, etc. This will give your organization both <u>practice using project structure</u> and <u>intimate knowledge of a Technical Readiness facilitating process</u> within it.

Chapter 9: Roles and responsibilities

No matter how structured or loose your methodology all work will be performed by team members who have roles and responsibilities. Project teams can be grouped into two broad categories:

- Core team members: Usually the people who do day-to-day work, coordination, project management. Core team members can have enduring roles or short, limited roles, e.g. electricians come in to install circuit boxes, circuits, etc. then exit the project work.

- Extended team members: Sponsors, stakeholders, interested parties, vendors that may be involved, consultants, etc.

Each team member serves a role, with some roles being more influential than others. The sponsor and project manager are the two key roles which have most of the power, influence, budget, responsibility and accountability.

The mobility and traction of work in your organization will depend on the degree of definition and support for these project roles

Project manager

The role and authority of project managers will vary depending on your reporting structure and where both the PM and project team members fit. However, I'd like you to consider roles and authority from the standpoint of completing work. <u>If the main objective is to add value by completing work, then regardless of reporting structure, what authority should the PM have within your organization?</u>

I take the position that the PM should have full authority to manage projects to complete the work and add value. Even to the point of telling other executives things like: "That request is not aligned with the goals and scope of the project so, no we won't do that."

PMs should be personally accountable to manage the project, reporting to the project sponsor, and stakeholders. Develop criteria for selecting or hiring project managers. If they are going to be personally accountable and you will need to support them, you better have PMs that are respected by others and are easy to support. Being blunt, selecting people who are popular, have internal relationships, etc. but are not competent nor respected by others, you are setting yourself up for contention. Select people who are a "total package" of competence, technical skills, speaking and leading teams, organized, able to lead others, etc. Are you ready for the other shoe to drop?

Hmmm. In order to have this authority and accountability the PM role must be supported through your entire chain of command. This is crucial. What factors are required for the PM to have the best opportunity for success?

Some project managers are not brought into projects until well after initiation and sometimes not until after scope definition. I take the position that PMs should be assigned and involved as soon as the idea for a project is considered. Many organizations make the mistake of not doing this. **Project Managers are the only role intimately involved with all aspects of projects**. This perspective allows them to think of how to manage and to begin organizing how to complete the work; from idea to reality. Assign project managers as early as possible and charge them with the responsibility to lead the project through all phases.

Second, PMs need the formal authority in order to have the responsibility. PMs can only control if they have the authority. In fact, I say that **PMs only have the authority which is supported by the highest executive.** Why? Because ultimately, someone will challenge this authority and the challenge will be escalated. If the PMs authority is supported at the highest level, then everyone knows the outcome before it is escalated. However, similarly but with an outcome against the PM if their authority is not supported. In which case, the PM is always working from a position of weakness and their decisions will reflect this. Neither is good for the added value your work is intended to provide.

Not having the authority means work needs to be completed but others can meddle in the project by altering scope, removing workers, changing priorities for team members. This leaves the PM with the responsibility but not the control. Sounds like a Dilbert to me. In the meantime, if the work and its representative value were a person, what do you think it would be saying and doing? Probably something like:

- What is my priority?
- I thought you wanted me by next month.
- I'm friends with team members Sal, Bobbi-Jo, and Kenzie so, if you take them away now a new team will need several weeks before they know me as well.

In order for PMs to have the authority, you and others in your organization must relinquish control to the PM and your project processes. Oh, you'll retain sponsor control so, you could shut down the project or reassign project managers if they aren't managing according to the plans, but you must relinquish operational control to the project manager and you must follow your project processes. Not doing this places the work and its value to your organization at risk of reduced value. Please note: This is inherent within a work ethic to add value.

Something to consider: PMs actually want to be held accountable. They want to develop the work, calculate and present metrics, manage changes, issues, risks. They want to delegate authority to those who will perform the work and hold them accountable for telling the PM about issues they need resolved. Unfortunately, in reality many executives and sponsors expect PMs to become involved in low level details. Doing this begins a vicious cycle that obstructs managing by metrics and enforcing the formal plans. The cycle flows like this:

- PMs get caught up in too much of the daily details that they simply run out of time.

- The desire by executives and stakeholders to know daily details or to become involved in the PMs authority begins to confuse which information and which metrics are important. Daily status details, e.g. "has that issue been worked out yet", become substitutes for meaningful cost and schedule metrics.

- Reports and status meetings become discussions of details that are best managed by supervisors, foremen and those doing the work. This changes the expectations of future discussions, leads to new metrics, charts and progress of things that really don't help manage the project.

Does a slogan come to mind? How about "Plan the work, then work the plan." Others?

Now consider relinquishing control to the project processes. By this I mean that even you should follow the established change management process, procurement process, human resources process, etc. Practically, if you or another executive want the project to finish earlier, complete more work, do the same work with fewer people and budget…then you must request these things following the appropriate processes.

But why? You are the executives. Are these not things executives are tasked to do? Maybe but remember two things:

1. You already chartered the project to complete a defined set of work – the scope.

2. Based on that scope the project team spent a lot of time figuring out how to complete the work. Therefore, the project schedule, costs, etc. reflect reality.

So introducing change creates a new reality; a reality that must be analyzed and a new reality determined that reflects the changes. My advocating that executives relinquish control to the project processes should be considered a way to protect the value you want delivered from any project, rather than considered a challenge to your role or authority.

Sponsors

By now you probably realize that sponsors must be strong partners with the project manager and the extended project team. Sponsors also must be advocates and champions of the project, yet not micromanage. OK, you also know that sponsors need to relinquish control to PMs. Sponsors need to ensure that the work to Initiate, Define Scope and Plan are performed thoroughly and are accepted by all other extended team members and others who have vested interest in the project.

While the PM should be involved from inception to lead the work, executives as sponsors are needed to frame the goals, objectives and deliverables from a business or operational perspective. I've seen many examples of projects providing status reports midway through development only to have executive sponsors ask "Why is the project doing these things? These are not why the project was chartered!" In most cases the scope was not hijacked or twisted intentionally. Mostly these are cases where executives as sponsors were not active advocates. They did not take time to meet with others, make presentations and provide enough education. As a result, all the others involved in scope definition and planning did not realize they were deviating from the real operational objectives. In my other book, "Project Management for Executives and Those Who Want to Influence Executives", the importance of active engagement by Executives is presented in detail.

I've also seen and experienced PMs try to maintain the sponsors' intended project scope but lose to stakeholders who understood the scope differently. In one situation a project team was midway through developing a solution, when a stakeholder cleverly intervened and redirected scope that changed the budget from under $100K to close to $1 million. The PM could not get the support needed, not even to use the approved change control processes to adjust scope and cost. Eventually, the PM was replaced by another who gave the stakeholder what they wanted. About a year later, after others saw the solution in operation, the entire solution was negated and superseded because it was not strategically nor operationally sound. In fact, developing consensus for the defined goals and deliverables of the project is another great example of the importance of soft skills. The core initial step in most facilitating processes is defining the topic. For projects, this includes goals and deliverables. Also in this case, the executive sponsor was not actively engaged to support the PM trying to resist the change.

Sponsors have a key role in providing the authority PMs need to manage projects, as they are chartered, defined and planned. Sponsors should advocate for projects up the executive chain of authority. I have also seen and been involved with sponsors who did this superbly. One project was originally approved for 1,500 hours and through a series of discoveries and cost-benefit analyses grew to 15,000 hours. The executive sponsor and his team partnered with the PM to present circumstances and options three different times to Vice Presidents; all were approved. The project was completed successfully with substantial value to the organization.

Sponsors also have a key role in determining who are stakeholders. I know that as project manager any sponsor-approved stakeholders are recognized by the people who chartered the work, fund the work and will benefit directly from the work. More about stakeholders below.

Stakeholders

I reinforce stakeholder involvement with this visual metaphor: "Stakeholders get to yank my PM chain, while interested parties do not." Again, <u>stakeholders approved by the sponsor have a direct vested interest in the project</u>.

These stakeholders should have subject matter experts assigned to the project, who help determine deliverables, requirements, controls, etc. So yes, stakeholders approved by the sponsor can yank my chain. This does not mean PMs lose their autonomy. Stakeholders can't change scope without formal change management. They can influence the management plans. For example, stakeholders can say:

"Your project is just not communicating to the community well. We are getting a lot of calls and meeting requests for information that should be coming from the project. Let's improve the communication plan with some bi-weekly press releases."

In fact, I recommend that the project charter specify which areas of your organization are accepted as stakeholders. If not then many people could request to be stakeholders and influence the work inappropriately. Perhaps adding a lot of nonessential work that distracts team members. Death by a thousand cuts. I advocate that if the sponsor does not include stakeholders in the Charter or after a request for stakeholders has circulated through the organization, that adding stakeholders must follow the change request process. I have irritated many people who wanted to be stakeholders to projects, but who were not listed as stakeholders in the project charter. In fact, just taking the stand that these people needed to discuss their involvement with the sponsors - in case this was an oversight - stopped their efforts and prevented unnecessary complications. I needed to rebuild some relationships, but protected the projects.

This may seem trivial but it really is crucial to creating a successful project management work environment. Think about it. Areas of your organization that have a legitimate stakeholder role should be considered when the work is chartered. If an area is missed or their importance is identified later, then the change request process is almost a done deal, but the request and approval provide formal documentation that they now get to influence the project or yank the PM's chain.

Interested parties

Interested parties may need to know project goals, objectives, deliverables, schedules, etc. because they need to prepare their organization or team. This may be a call center team that needs to add staff and attend training in time to support the new functionality. This may be an area that wants to benefit from lessons-learned or see your metrics so they can brainstorm their own. They may be planning upgrades to their processes or want to learn the most recent legislative rules that your project is pioneering.

Interested parties do not get to yank my chain. However, interested parties can be influential allies in your organization. They may be able to influence others, trade returned budget money to your sponsor in return for a player to be named later, etc.

Key point is that parts of your organization will be interested parties. Invite them to meetings. Allow them to see documents. Keep them informed via formal and informal discussions. They will need to work through proper channels if they want to upgrade to becoming a stakeholder, but they should be welcomed, extended team members.

Core team

The core team includes team members who have substantial subject matter knowledge, understand what is needed to actually perform the work and who have the experience for an end-to-end view. In most organizations the core team includes:

- Project managers
- Team Leads, supervisors, foremen, i.e. those who lead others who do the work.
- Coordinators who work closely to lead sub-efforts or bridge between the project and the rest of the organization.

The core team works with the PM to plan the work and execute the management plans. Some organizations and projects are small enough that all project team members are on the core team. That is quite reasonable.

Core team members should attend all project status meetings, contribute to metric reporting, identify risks, issues and other factors that affect the work.

Extended team

The extended team includes those people who actually do the work. Some may be vendors who pop in for a few days then leave. Others may have an oversight role to ensure company policies and procedures are followed. Of course these policies and procedures should be included with the management plans. All this is good.

A note about work assignments and capacity management

While this is not a role, this is an appropriate place to reinforce People Management from Chapter 5 for assigning work and for monitoring your organization's work capacity from Chapter 7 Metrics. I encourage you to reread these sections. Discuss capacity openly and honestly to determine a commitment to using your employees wisely and committing to only the work for which your organization has capacity. Oh, and remember that this needs to include the amount of time they spend correcting defects from previous projects.

Chapter 10: Create your future

As a kid did you ever climb on top of a teeter-totter and try to balance it by straddling the fulcrum? Ever try tight-rope walking or walking on top of a barrel? I think sometimes adults lose the memory of active and physical challenges like these. As my kids were growing up and I took them to a park across the street, I'd steal some time for myself and try tight-rope walking on some rope nets strung in a spider web design with inclines and tight angles and varying tensions. I progressed slowly from standing for more than a nanosecond to a couple of steps to half a section and so on. After many months I sometimes could traverse several sections easily. The next trip I again was falling off after only a couple of steps. My kids are grown and I now live in the country far from the park. I still want to learn to ride a unicycle because I like the challenge and reminder of the balance, the tension between control and loss of control.

I want you to know that the challenge of finding and maintaining the balance and control of managing work in your organization is similar to walking a tight rope, walking on top of a barrel or straddling a teeter-totter. Muscles provide strength and active adjustments while joints flex to absorb excess energy and motion and maintain your center of gravity. You are now at the point of jumping on the rope, establishing balance, control and traversing from points A to B.

How to implement an environment using project management principles

I recommend running a project to implement this type of work culture change. You could run an additional project each year for 2-3 years, that pilots some specific functionality, tools and processes. Consider the value of implementing a new environment through formal projects.

- All aspects of project management will be experienced and reinforced within your organization. Real, practical experience.

- This experience will lead to customizations that fit your organization and the nature of your work.

- Your organization can determine which operations can be implemented first, second, etc. This will include easy wins.

- Your organization can gain experience with facilitating processes as you analyze situations, make decisions, develop work breakdown structures, WBS dictionaries and work task schedules.

- The culture changes will be more evolutionary than revolutionary and your staff will be aware of what, why and how the changes will be made.

I could continue, but you get the point.

Knowing where to begin

How will you know the right level to begin? How can you plan so that you know how well you've done and how to advance to the next level? My guideline is what I call the Least Level of Intrusion Model or getting the most benefit for the least disruption.

Start with the least amount of newness or intrusion your organization can incorporate for several projects. Learn from these. Let your organization become familiar with the processes, controls, terms and results. Oh, and implement metrics to track results.

Progress at the pace and with the activities your organization requests. You'll know this from comments like: "You know, those check points weren't as bad as I thought." "That sponsor usually changes their mind and gets their way, but they couldn't do it this time." "The risk rating chart really helped me understand that something I thought was trivial was really important."

Create a framework

I recommend starting with these five components because they represent the most <u>control</u> for the least intrusion. If you read my book "Project Management for Executives and Those Who Want to Influence Executives" you'll see this presented with more detail, but the essence is the same.

1. Develop a framework that can be used on several projects. This should be straight forward and uncomplicated. Include:
    a. An Initiating Phase that produces a Charter.
    b. A Planning Phase that produces a master plan with scope, change and risk management plans.
    c. Communications reports for weekly status meetings and periodic sponsor and stakeholder meetings.
2. Use the facilitating processes that seem to make sense. I recommend highly:
    a. Rules for effective meetings
    b. WBS Discovery exercise.
    c. Situation analysis.
    d. Decision making.
3. Use a methodology that focuses on discrete deliverables within defined timeframes. Again, SCRUM and Rolling Wave accommodate this well.
4. Use tools from the appendix or other sources you think can add the most value. I recommend:
    a. The Risk rating tool.
    b. The Requirements Traceability Matrix.
5. Implement a staff capacity and allocation process.

Again, these can be implemented via a project to create a project management work environment.

Lessons learned

Lessons Learned seems fairly self-explanatory, i.e. a discussion of events leading to identification of lessons that can be applied to your organization. Lessons Learned may never benefit your organization if they are not managed effectively. I have seen repeatedly Lessons Learned discussed, compiled, documented then never to be resurrected or used.

I want to share a real story that reinforces my perspective of how Lessons Learned should be managed. The presenter at a project management seminar in Springfield, IL was a 30-year plus career project manager as a government contractor. He said: "I can tell you 10 Lessons Learned before a project even begins."

Wow! I could not have asked for a better lead to make my point during the Q & A period: That documenting Lessons Learned are not enough. Unless Lessons Learned are actually assigned as tasks to specific people with a date for completion, the benefit will probably never be realized. Someone needs to have ownership and be accountable for implementation."

Here is a sample Lessons Learned table you can use. It is also included in the appendix.

Table 6: Lessons Learned Table Sample

Situation	Lesson Learned	Who is Assigned	Expected Action and Date	Additional Notes
Two requirements were not identified until testing / inspection because the team lead did not have sufficient subject matter knowledge.	Work is complex enough that technicians who will be assigned need to be involved with requirements analysis.	Unit managers Shelly Anderson and Philipe Herrera. Director Catherine Bailey.	Update list of unit activity assignments to include at least one technician for requirements analysis. By next project.	This assignment becomes part of unit managers' yearly performance review to be conducted by their Director.
Flooring contractor notified PM of issues with the work order preventing rework and a two week delay.	Rewarding contractor with a percent of cost-of-consequences resulted in net cost saving. Reinforce this practice.	Procurement Division Senior Attorney.	Update all procurement templates, including SOWs and Contractor Expectations. By Q3 this year.	PMs should continue to document these situations in their "Value of Finding Defects Early" document so they can be tracked by project.

Notice how this type of approach actually integrates lessons that can add value. In the first example, the assignment becomes part of managers' performance reviews and in doing so their boss becomes aware in a way that is measurable. In the second example a contractor has incentive to raise awareness of potential problems. This is part of instilling the ethic that they are part of an extended team to add value to your organization.

I also encourage you to make Lessons Learned review a component of Executive year-end reviews. This way they'll know this activity actually provides value and it will serve as input to your organization's strategic planning.

Value of finding defects early

I want to expound on the second Lessons Learned example of the value of finding defects early. This could have been added to Chapter 6: Metrics, but I thought it would have more punch if presented as part of Creating Your Future. Every industry can benefit from identifying or finding defects early, whether building a bridge, developing a new engine, or planning for a national sales team annual meeting. In Information Technology, estimates of the cost of finding defects during different stages of software development vary widely. For this topic I use values that are within a reasonable range.

The following tool used within appropriate work activities provides several benefits.

- All participants are encouraged to think end-to-end and out of the box.

- Reinforcing the value of working smart first, hard second.

- All project team members see the relationship of previous to successive work stages.

- All project team members can be recognized and rewarded for contributing value. In fact, a monetary value can be attributed to their contributions.

A couple of notes. During Initiation and Requirements Development this activity does not necessarily identify defects, but does identify omissions, poorly stated goals, objectives and requirements that can lead to unintended deliverables and defects during later stages. Rather than quibble about what is and is not a defect, emphasize to your teams that the purpose is to add value by working smart first and hard second.

Here is the tool. A blank template is in the appendix. How it works is described below the tool.

Table 7: Tool for Measuring the Value of Finding Defects Early vs. Late Sample

Phase	Requirements	Design	Build	Test	Implemented / Supported
Cost at phase	$50	$250	$1,000	$2,500	$5,000
Potential value	$5,000	$5,000	$5,000	$5,000	$5,000
Credited value at phase	$5,000 - $50 = $4,950	$5,000 - $250 = $4,750	$5,000 - $1,000 = $4,000	$5,000 - $2,500 = $2,500	$5,000 - $5,000 = $0
Person/ Phase	**Requirements**	**Design**	**Build**	**Test**	**Implemented / Supported**
Phil	5 X $4,950 = $24,750				
Renee		2 X $4,750 = $9,500	2 X $4,750 = $9,500		
Jon				10 X $2,500 = $25,000	
Costs post-implementation					5 X $5,000 = $25,000
Defect prevention value at phase.	$24,750	$9,500	$9,500	$25,000	$0
Cumulative team defect prevention	$24,750	$34,250	$43,750	$68,750	$68,750 - $25,000 = $43,750

The top section presents work phases as four columns. The rows present

1. The assumed cost of correcting an error at that time/ phase.

2. The potential value of not needing to fix a problem in production. Fixing a problem always costs. In this case -$5,000 if it reaches production. So, fixing it before production represents a positive $5,000 of value minus the cost of fixing it during a previous phase.

3. The credited value of catching the error or defect at that phase.

The assumed cost of correcting an error once a deliverable is completed, i.e. implemented and supported, equals $5,000. Catching it during Requirements only costs $50 so the potential value is $5,000 minus $50 = $4,950. This makes sense because the cost of requirements involves meetings, discussions and document reviews for a fairly low investment cost. However, if errors, omissions or defects are not caught until a deliverable is being produced the assumed cost is much higher because the impact affects so much more than just meetings and document reviews. In this case the assumed cost of correcting an error during the Build phase is $2,500, so the potential value is $5,000 - $2,500 = $2,500; much less than catching the error during requirements.

OK, the rows following the top four are to credit team members for their contributions during each phase. Phil found five errors during requirements for a total credited value of $24,750. Renee was involved during design and build where she found four errors for a total credited value of $19,000. The post-implementation costs equal five defects at a cost of $5,000 each for a total of $25,000.

The last two rows show the value of preventing defects at each work phase and the cumulative value by phase and post-implementation, respectively. Even though the team would have preferred to catch the post-implementation defects earlier, the total value of catching defects early is still a positive $43,750.

Now being a sharp person, you probably have several questions and objections to the cost assumptions and whether a tool like this can reflect reality. I agree, but hear me out. If you don't already have a method to collect these type of metrics, then this is a useful tool to begin. As you track the time spent by your project teams during each phase and use the rigor of project management principles, your organization will be able to collect fairly accurate and meaningful metrics that can be plugged into this or a similar tool. At that point, your organization will have a critical mass of data to provide even better evidence of the value for working smart first, hard second.

A note about team spirit and camaraderie. Jon being a tester should not feel bad that he does not contribute as much to the potential value simply because his assignment is closer to implementation. In fact, he gets bragging rights over Phil and Renee because he found things during Testing that slipped through them.

Also, customer service or - whichever part of your organization handles post-implementation issues - is often overlooked during initiation, planning and requirements development. An effective project management work environment should include them during each phase. Their perspective can really add value because they can recognize things that affect them thereby helping prevent errors and defects. This follows the adage:

- The least expensive service call or activity is the one that is not made.

Think of the Maytag repairman commercials. Your organization will need teams to manage post-implementation issues, but their best value is when they are not busy.

Closing Comments

I requested reviews from colleagues who work in various industries during book development and the feedback was always constructive and led to improvements. When the book was in the "minor tweaking" stage I was working with Stan – a big guy with a bright and infectious smile. We worked together for about five months and talked about how to improve our operations enough that I felt comfortable asking if he would like to read the book. A couple of weeks later he said, "I've read enough to think that you took a lot from this place." I replied, "Actually, I've added less than 1% since I started working here with you." His smile seemed to glow as he said "Pretty common, huh?"

I felt confident that the book was ready because Stan could see all around him what the book presents; the very good and things that needed improvement. He felt it identified his situations. I hope now that you've read it, you feel the same.

So where to go from here!

An important goal of this book is to present ways to influence your organization. Ways to get employees to understand how they can work smarter. A question I asked all reviewers is: "Do you think the active exercises and slogans are appropriate and could be used in your work environment?" Most reviewers thought they could with this caveat: "We've never done this sort of thing before, so I don't know how it would be received."

DO NOT LET THIS DETER OR DELAY YOU! USE THESE AND OTHER ACTIVE EXERCISES!

Organizational change only happens if the change reaches a critical mass that can then self generate. Using this book among a small group of people is a good start but will not result in reaching that critical mass. That also requires a plan to get your people thinking and talking. Get them to the point where they are willing to try new things and discussing what worked, what did not, and to challenge each other to think in terms of adding value. Get your executives to the point where they are willing to give up control to a project team, feeling confident that the framework for success is so strong that the project team can succeed with oversight and light touches, but not intrusion.

Appendix

Appendix A: Notes and Implementation Ideas

Chapter	Topic	Note / Idea / Question	Implementation Idea
Chapter 1			
Chapter 2			
Chapter 3			
Chapter 4			
Chapter 5			
Chapter 6			
Chapter 7			
Chapter 8			
Chapter 9			
Chapter 10			

Appendix B: Sample Project Management Expectations and Assumptions Checklist

Project Management Expectations	Pros and Cons	Organizational Culture Impact	Ideas We Can Brainstorm
Project Management Assumptions	Pros and Cons	Organizational Culture Impact	Ideas We Can Brainstorm

Appendix C: Requirements Traceability Matrix Template

Requirement	Deliverables	Documents	Training	Testing	Approvals	WBS
R1	Tools					
	Screens					
	Calculation engines					
R2 Electronic Document Management	Hardware	Architecture				
	Software	Operations				
	Tiff images	Design/configuration				
	Trained staff	User & Admin. Guides				
R3 Backfile in format that does not change	Tiff images	Processes and procedures				
		QA processes				
		Metrics and reports				

Appendix D: WBS Dictionary

High level task	Low-level task / activity	Who performs: Vendor, client, other	Duration	Dependencies	Risks	Risk mitigation
Develop business process	Step 1	Vendor BA	40 hours / 5 days			
	Step 2	Client BA	10 hours / 2 days			
	Step 3	Sub TA	3 hours / 1 day			
	Step N					

Appendix E: Risk Tool

Risk	Probability of Occurring (1 = low to 10 = high)	Impact if Risk Occurs (1 = low to 10 = high)	Total Risk Rating (Probability X Impact)	Mitigation Options
Vendor has only produced low volumes. Supply and quality could be unacceptable.	3	10	30	Project is purchasing new, high-volume equipment. Assist vendor to determine and measure quality as volume is increased.

Appendix F: Decision Analysis / Pugh Matrix

Decision Analysis Matrix Sample

Decision Objective: Select a new LOB application

Key: Precise statement. No ambiguity. Objective evaluation and selection

Objectives	Must or Want	Want Value (1-10)	Option A — Meet Must	Option A — Want Rating (1-10)	Option A — Want Percent (score X Want value)	Option B — Meet Must	Option B — Want Rating (1-10)	Option B — Want Percent (score X Want value)	Option C — Meet Must	Option C — Want Rating (1-10)	Option C — Want Percent (score X Want value)
Browser based	Must		Yes		0	No		0	Y		0
Compatible w/existing database	Must		Yes		0	Y		0	Y		0
Uses same database	Want	5		10	5 * 10 = 50		0	5 * 0 = 0		5	5 * 5 = 25
Individual letter generation	Must		Yes		0	Y		0	Y		0
Batch/mass letter generation	Must		Yes		0	Y		0	Y		0
Configurable calculation engine	Want	9		6	9 * 6 = 54		7	9 * 7 =63		0	9 * 0 = 0
Standard actuarial formulas	Must		Yes		0	Y		0	Y		0
Create custom actuarial formulas	Want	8		5	8 * 5 = 40		10	8*10 = 80		7	8 * 7 = 56
Integrates w/time reporting system	Want	6		10	6 * 10 = 60		10	6 *10 = 60		6	6 * 6 = 36
MS-Windows Server system	Must		Yes		0	Y		0	Y		0
Security via Active Directory	Want	7		10	7 * 10 = 70		7	7 * 0 = 0		8	7 * 8 = 56
Security configurable by staff role	Must		Yes		0	No		0	Y		0
Score	Want	350 (Perfect Score)			274			203			173
Result					High Score			Eliminate: Two musts not met			Second
Conduct Risk/ Opportunity analysis					Low risk						Moderate risk
Final Decision					Preferred vendor						Alternate vendor

Appendix G: Technical Readiness Level Descriptions

TRL 1 Basic principles observed and reported: Transition from scientific research to applied research. Essential characteristics and behaviors of systems and architectures. Descriptive tools are mathematical formulations or algorithms.

TRL 2 Technology concept and/or application formulated: Applied research. Theory and scientific principles are focused on specific application area to define the concept. Characteristics of the application are described. Analytical tools are developed for simulation or analysis of the application.

TRL 3 Analytical and experimental critical function and/or characteristic proof-of concept: Proof of concept validation. Active Research and Development (R&D) is initiated with analytical and laboratory studies. Demonstration of technical feasibility using breadboard or brassboard implementations that are exercised with representative data.

TRL 4 Component/subsystem validation in laboratory environment: Standalone prototyping implementation and test. Integration of technology elements. Experiments with full-scale problems or data sets.

TRL 5 System/subsystem/component validation in relevant environment: Thorough testing of prototyping in representative environment. Basic technology elements integrated with reasonably realistic supporting elements. Prototyping implementations conform to target environment and interfaces.

TRL 6 System/subsystem model or prototyping demonstration in a relevant end-to-end environment (ground or space): Prototyping implementations on full-scale realistic problems. Partially integrated with existing systems. Limited documentation available. Engineering feasibility fully demonstrated in actual system application.

TRL 7 System prototyping demonstration in an operational environment (ground or space): System prototyping demonstration in operational environment. System is at or near scale of the operational system, with most functions available for demonstration and test. Well integrated with collateral and ancillary systems. Limited documentation available.

TRL 8 Actual system completed and "mission qualified" through test and demonstration in an operational environment (ground or space): End of system development. Fully integrated with operational hardware and software systems. Most user documentation, training documentation, and maintenance documentation completed. All functionality tested in simulated and operational scenarios. Verification and Validation (V&V) completed.

TRL 9 Actual system "mission proven" through successful mission operations (ground or space): Fully integrated with operational hardware/software systems. Actual system has been thoroughly demonstrated and tested in its operational environment. All documentation completed. Successful operational experience. Sustaining engineering support in place.

Appendix G: Value of Finding Defects Early Tool

Table 7: Value of Finding Defects Early Versus Late Tool.tif

Phase	Requirements	Design	Build	Test	Implemented / Supported
Cost	$50	$250	$1,000	$2,500	$5,000
Potential value	$5,000	$5,000	$5,000	$5,000	$5,000
Credited value	$5,000 - $50 = $4,950	$5,000 - $250 = $4,750	$5,000 - $1,000 = $4,000	$5,000 - $2,500 = $2,500	$5,000 - $5,000 = $0
Person/ Phase	Requirements	Design	Build	Test	Implemented / Supported

INDEX

R

S